"An excellent read. Through the fruits of his introspection, Dr. Angtuaco not only offers food for thought, but his meditations and perspectives within the biblical context offer nourishment for the interested readers' spirits."
-- *Dr. Johnny Jones, Gastroenterologist*

"This book is a brilliant blend of spiritual insights, psychology, and practical wisdom that will inspire and enrich your life. The author will help you find joy in the ordinary and strength to overcome everyday challenges you thought were insurmountable. Indeed, an invaluable resource for those searching for answers.
-- *Dr. Shawn Bao, Endocrinologist*

"Captivating, encouraging and relatable — this is a book you'll want to read daily to remind yourself how to bring light back into your soul. Dr. Angtuaco will motivate you to become the best version of yourself and seek an unwavering faith in God!"
-- *Clint Webb, BBA, Pharmaceutical Sales Representative*

"The author takes readers on a journey to seek answers through a faith-filled life. The stories contained in this book resonated with my soul in ways I could not have imagined. I often refer to this resource to help me find light in my everyday life."
-- *Allison Bermudez, Communications Consultant*

AuthorHouse™
1663 Liberty Drive
Bloomington, IN 47403
www.authorhouse.com
Phone: 833-262-8899

Published by AuthorHouse 12/04/2023

ISBN: 979-8-8230-1750-3 (sc)
ISBN: 979-8-8230-1749-7 (e)

Print information available on the last page.

Book Cover Image Credit: Cliff Pennington

This book is printed on acid-free paper.

SOUL TO SOUL
FINDING LIGHT IN MY EVERYDAY LIFE

BY
TERENCE ANGTUACO, M.D.

authorHOUSE®

I dedicate this book to my wife, Josephine, and our three children, Tyler, Julienne, and Jaymie. Your kindness to others inspired me, and your generous sacrifices allowed me to finish writing this book.

I appreciate the love, encouragement, and support of my family, friends, and patients. Thank you to those who trusted me and allowed me to comfort them during their most vulnerable moments. Helping you helped me become wiser and taught me to love better. I am grateful to those who shared their time and talent to help make this book one that I am truly proud of. To all of you, I dedicate this.

Acknowledgments

Book cover design by
Cliff Pennington

Editing and proofreading by
Travis Bond
Allison Bermudez

Author photograph by
Norman Bercasio Photography
www.normanbercasio.com

TABLE OF CONTENTS

INTRODUCTION

Each week for thirty consecutive weeks, I wrote about insights I gleaned from dealing with personal struggles during that period. Some of the topics covered in this book were inspired by conversations with family, close friends, and patients who shared their heartfelt stories and sought my advice and encouragement. These motivated me to look deeper into issues I would otherwise take for granted. I spent hours praying, meditating, and reflecting to discern lessons that could be learned. As I wrote about them, I gained clarity on the issues. This book was written with a specific reader in mind – me. It is my personal journal to help remind me how to deal with the same challenges I know will resurface in the future. I was a medical professor, and I held the dictum that I have not sufficiently learned a topic unless I can teach it. Now that I have completed writing this book, the next step is to practice what I have learned and strive to improve each day at living it.

I picked the title, *"Soul to Soul"* because I wrote everything in this book with all sincerity and vulnerability, putting aside any attempt to hide behind a façade of strength and security. I hope my readers will receive it with the same openness and allow the ideas to percolate their minds and tug their souls. If this book were to help encourage or inspire even just one person, all the time and effort I put into writing this would have been well worth it, and the book would have served the purpose I had hoped for.

In Luke 11:9, Jesus said, *"Ask and you will receive, seek and you will find."* I organized the book into ten parts, each representing a theme of something we aspire to. Each part starts with a prayer asking God to grant what I need, which I expect to receive as promised. The title of each part begins with the word "seeking." In each chapter under it, I shared wisdom I found as I searched for answers to questions I encountered in my everyday life. This may be used as a daily devotional with one chapter for each day of the month, or as a go-to book to provide inspiration and encouragement when experiencing a particular need.

I hope you will enjoy reading this book as much as I enjoyed writing it.

"And so I say to you: Ask, and you will receive; seek, and you will find; knock, and the door will be opened to you. For those who ask will receive, and those who seek will find, and the door will be opened to anyone who knocks."

LUKE 11:9-10 (GNTD)

PART I: SEEKING INNER PEACE

Dear God,

My heart is restless, and my mind is weary.

Help me be still and find calm within.

Grant me the kind of peace only You can give;

the kind our minds can only try to understand.

Chapter 1
Think Better, Feel Better

A group of psychologists at Queen's University in Canada, reported in July 2020 in *Nature Communications* that the human brain generated, on average, 6,200 thoughts per day. Presuming we are awake sixteen hours a day, that is an average of 387 thoughts per hour. If we dwell on all these thoughts and leave ourselves with no time to act on anything, we will accomplish nothing in life. Furthermore, if the thoughts were unpleasant, we would be left feeling depressed and discouraged. Each day, there are a lot of opportunities to become anxious, worried, stressed, angry, lonely, and hurt. They all start and end in our minds.

It is said, "*Sometimes less is more.*" We can think less of some things to gain more joy. We do not have to think about every thought that crosses our minds. We do not have to have an answer to every question in life. We do not have to defend ourselves against every accusation hurled at us. We do not have to correct every mistake we make in our lives. We do not have to finish every task and chore on our to-do list immediately. We do not have to try to solve every problem we face today. Just because we can does not mean we should. We do not need to face head on every obstacle we encounter in life; it is often wiser to just go around them.

Many of us sacrifice our joy and peace today because we focus on the past we cannot change and the future that is merely imagined. We erroneously judge the present based on past truths and false assumptions about the future. As a result, we lose the opportunity to make today a wonderful memory to cherish tomorrow.

Of course, we need to constantly reflect, ponder, analyze, and strategize to succeed in our endeavors, overcome challenges, and appreciate the beauty of life. That is why we educate and enlighten ourselves. The Greek philosopher Socrates once said, *"The unexamined life is not worth living."* Thinking is not the problem; what we choose to think about and how we manage our thoughts will determine whether we become wiser and happier or fruitless and despondent.

In Philippians 4:8, St. Paul said, *"Whatever is true, whatever is noble, whatever is right, whatever is pure, whatever is lovely, whatever is admirable—if anything is excellent or praiseworthy—think about such things."* This biblical truth can help us filter our daily stream of thoughts into our minds.

Some thoughts are for us to cherish and enjoy. Others are for us to process and act on. Many are mere distractions that come to us like dust, and we should treat them as such and just let them pass. We can lose ourselves tracking the specks of dust if we are not careful. The dust can hypnotize us into oblivion, and we soon realize how much time we lost that we can never get back. It is important to live consciously and be purposeful in what we do. We miss so much beauty in our lives because we sleepwalk through it. We take things for granted because we have so many blessings, they become ordinary. The ability to multi-task has become a badge of honor, but its perceived advantage is a delusion. We lose more than we think we gain. In this era of multi-tasking and easy access to various modes of electronic communication, our relationships and social interactions have become more superficial and less meaningful. Living consciously requires us to be mentally present in whatever it is we are doing. If we are driving, we must focus on the lines that mark our lanes and the cars around us. Drinking coffee, eating a meal, talking on the phone, or answering texts while driving is not only dangerous, but exhausting. When talking to someone, we need to listen attentively and actively engage in the conversation. We miss the opportunity to learn and connect deeper if we are focused on saying our piece while the other person is talking. Doing mundane things consciously like brushing our teeth and combing our hair can be a calming experience. Being aware of the movements of our chest and abdomen with each breath, and the movements of our limbs as we walk, can help us appreciate God's blessings of life and health that we would otherwise take for granted.

When there are challenges that our minds cannot process or solve, I find it best just to let them go for the moment and reconsider later. Dwelling on it does not fix the problem; it wears you down. Over the years, I realized that everything in life eventually takes care of itself one way or another. Everything in life is temporary, both good and bad. Robert Plant wrote a song about a Persian king who etched a caption on his ring that says, *"Even this shall pass away,"* to remind him that everything in life is fleeting and not to be attached to anything. Every problem eventually works itself out in the end. My confidence comes from believing that God is in control of the universe. I know when all is said and done, all will be well. Everything God allows in our lives serves a purpose. I have experienced God's unimaginable love enough to know He will always help me overcome. I expect once the storm passes, as I pick up the pieces, I will feel closer to God. I will become a better person because of the transformational experience of the storm. God can now use the thousands of shattered pieces of me to serve thousands more people at a time. In Jeremiah 29:11, God said, *"For I know the plans I have for you. Plans to prosper you and not to harm you, plans to give you hope and a future."* If we have God in our lives, we can rest easy and surrender our anxious thoughts to Him. In Isaiah 26:3, it says that God will keep in perfect peace all who trust in Him and all whose thoughts are fixed on Him.

CHAPTER 2
LET GO AND BE TRULY FREE

"It is for freedom that Christ has set us free. Stand firm, then, and do not let yourselves be burdened again by a yoke of slavery." Galatians 5:1

The sun rises and sets whether we want it to or not. Things happen and circumstances change whether we like it or not; many of which we cannot predict. Nothing stays the same. Everything is temporary, and everyone is transient. Aging is a good example. We resist it, dread it, and sometimes, deny it, but we can never stop it. We become anxious and unhappy when we refuse to accept things as they are. What we need to strive for is the ability to let go of "what was" and let "what is" be. The process of letting go is often gradual. It is a conscious decision that is executed rationally.

Beauty fades, physical strength diminishes, and mental acuity dulls. Wealth, health, and power can be here today and gone tomorrow. Relationships can be warm and satisfying for a period and then stale and superficial over time. We should expect and learn to accept these realities, let go of what's gone, and make the most of what we have now. We must be open to new ways of dealing with unfamiliar conditions, even uncomfortable ones. It is nice to cherish the past, but we cannot let it anchor us to a period that no longer exists and cannot be altered. We should seek beauty in the present and enjoy every moment of it. Like crustaceans and reptiles who constantly shed and replace their outer layers, we should always be willing to let go of what was or had been and accept what is here and now. Like a butterfly, we should allow the natural process of metamorphosis to transform us from a caterpillar to a beautiful, winged insect. Give yourself a chance to be pleasantly surprised by where reality leads you. We must continually adapt, reinvent ourselves, make new friends, and keep seeking our evolving purpose in life.

Do not hold on too tightly to anything or anyone. Do not define yourself based on what you possess or achieved. What will become of you when these things meet their expiration date? This does not mean you do not give your best and seek success. We are expected to maximize our potential using all the talents God gave us. We are expected to love deeply and work hard to nurture the relationships God blessed us with. Avoiding the pain of losing something or someone is not a justifiable reason to shun being fully dedicated to a cause or investing emotionally in another person. The regret of not doing what you know you can do or should do can be more painful. Instead, be fully committed to everything, and be sincere with everyone. But be mindful that all we have gained and acquired are gifts from God. They were given to us for a reason and may only be needed for a season. Once God has achieved His purpose, He may take them away. When that time comes, we must be willing to let go with faith and accept God's will.

When we hold on to the success we once had, the person we once were, past hurts and mistakes, relationships that have gone cold, and addictions we think we could not live without, we are like a hot air balloon that would not rise because of the weight that holds it down. They keep us from truly being free and becoming the person God intended us to be. Ultimately, they keep us from achieving happiness and success. Each day, we should avoid hoarding hurts, holding on to unnecessary baggage, and bringing home trash other people throw at us. Acknowledge the past and manage the present. Let go of what you should and wait on God. Trust Him to help you navigate the difficult moments. Do not resist and just let life play out like it was meant to be, and you will know how it feels to be truly free.

"Acknowledge the past and manage the present. Let go of what you should and wait on God."

CHAPTER 3
STICK TO WHAT IS TRUE

Sometimes, one's perception of a situation is real only in his mind. This could lead to unnecessary hurts and unfulfilled expectations. For example, a close friend who usually sends a text or calls every day failed to do so. You happened to feel unwell that day and wished someone had checked on you. You interpreted what happened as evidence your friend did not care. Worse, you jumped to conclude that your friend never was true to you. Your mind made a giant leap from the only fact you had, which was your friend's failure to send a text or call, to a damaging unproven conclusion that he was insincere. Imagine the suffering you must have endured because of this.

Jesus said in John 8:32, *"You will know the truth, and the truth will set you free."* Although Jesus was alluding to a higher spiritual truth, this teaching applies to many levels of our lives. Often, the truth, no matter how dire, does not cause as much suffering as our opinion of the truth and assumptions of its implications. In the above example, the only truth was you did not receive the text or call you expected. That, in and of itself, was harmless and neutral. What was hurtful and damaging was the baseless conclusion you made that you were misled all these years and your friend was unworthy. This negativity undoubtedly can lead to more negative thoughts in the future. This perceived betrayal made you believe this will happen again and possibly worse. Let us try a more severe example. What if you were diagnosed with a serious illness, like cancer? When you heard what the doctor told you, the only truth you had at the time was you had cancer. As I am sure this was devastating news, the expected response would be to think how awful this was, how difficult surgery and/or chemotherapy would be, and how little time you had left. These responses are your opinion of the facts you just received and the assumptions you made. You labeled cancer as awful, which it is. You assumed that treatment would be difficult and interpreted a cancer diagnosis as the end of everything. All your responses were appropriate, but not all your assumptions were true. You then felt horrible and suffered deeply. There was no doubt it would be overwhelming to receive a diagnosis of cancer. As bad as the situation was, there was no need to make it worse. The goal was to cope and have peace despite the odds. You cannot deny the truth. Hence, you should accept it. But be sure to focus only on what was true at the moment. The truth was the diagnosis you received. Your opinion about the truth was what troubled you. Having this insight helps you avoid unnecessary suffering. We need to learn to accept the truth and forgo the opinion. Should your worst fear become a reality, you will deal with the new truth in the same manner; you will acknowledge it, accept it, fix what you can, let go of what you cannot, and rest in the hope your faith brings.

Your interpretation of a situation is often influenced by your emotional state at the time of its occurrence. It is dangerous to be led solely by your emotions. There is an acronym H.A.L.T. which stands for Hungry, Angry, Lonely, and Tired. This acronym is used as a check-in process for rehabilitating addicts to avoid specific triggers for relapse. They are reminded to stop (or halt) and think before pursuing a thought when they are hungry, angry, lonely, or tired. This reminder can also help you avoid drawing incorrect conclusions about a situation or making bad decisions when in a compromised emotional state.

More than success, wealth, and health, I yearn for peace of mind and wish the same for the people I love. If I have peace, I have true happiness. To achieve this, we must focus on just the truth. We process numerous thoughts each day, and many are unnecessary and toxic. In one of the examples above, if you had acknowledged only the fact at hand, that you did not receive a text or call from someone who usually does, and left it at that, you would have kept your peace. That is what was true then, and that is all that mattered. What you thought might have been why it did not happen, need not be entertained as it was unverified. What your friend did in the past should also not matter. What you think your friend might become in the future should not matter as well. I know this is a seemingly shallow and inconsequential example, but these are the little sufferings that consume us daily. They damage our psyche and mental health more than the rare major life events. It is important to remember that it is not reality that robs us of our joy, it is our misrepresentation of reality that does. In this example, what if your friend could not call because he was deathly ill? That was not something that you would have known at the time. The reverse can be true that your friend could have also been disappointed that you failed to be there for him in his time of need. If we take things at face value and adhere to the truth we know for sure and do not dabble in second guesses and assumptions based on past experiences, we could spare ourselves a lot of unnecessary pain. As soon as I say this, I am sure some may think, "What if this happens repeatedly?" That question is not about a fact but a possibility; it is about the future. We should live in the present, deal with what we know today, trust that God will meet our needs, and be concerned about the future only when it becomes the here and now. We should always focus on acknowledging only what we are sure is true. Let the truth speak for itself, and do not editorialize the truth. In the end, we will realize that life isn't too bad after all.

Chapter 4
It Takes Three to Tango

You want to live in peace. You forgive people who may or may not deserve it and even reward them despite their misdeeds, just to preserve your peace of mind. Sometimes, "winning the battle" is not worth losing your peace. Others around you may think it is irrational to let people get away with their mischief. They constantly criticize you for this and cause more turmoil than what you are trying to avoid in the first place. They want you to confront and punish those who deserve it; to exact the same "eye for an eye and a tooth for a tooth" kind of vengeance with which they are familiar. You feel lost and your mind is weary, and realize you failed in your quest for peace.

You want a mutually loving and considerate relationship, but the other person does not define loving and considerate the way you do. Despite this, you continue to invest into the relationship that which you hope to receive. Nothing changes and you begin to feel this is one-sided despite your efforts. The quality of your time together diminishes, and you begin to feel distant. Over time, you become uncertain of the reasons the relationship even began.

Things do not always work out in life the way we desire. We are all interdependent, and the outcome of our efforts depends on the contributions of others and our circumstances. It really takes more than two to tango. There is you, and there is the other person. You do your best to achieve what you want in life, but you also need those around you to cooperate to succeed. Circumstances also affect how things turn out. Sometimes people who reliably act one way surprise you with an uncharacteristic response to a situation. Occasionally, a seemingly hopeless situation turns around without any effort on your part. So, who controls these circumstances? Who is the third party in this dance? It is God. In Psalms 127:1-2, it says, *"Unless the Lord builds the house, the builders labor in vain. Unless the Lord watches over the city, the guards stand watch in vain. In vain you rise early and stay up late, toiling for food to eat."* It takes your effort, other people's willingness to cooperate, and God's blessings to make things happen. Life is a dance among these three parties.

Although it takes three to tango, you can control only one. You cannot change the thoughts or behaviors of another, and you cannot control God; you can only control and change yourself. Spare yourself the frustration of trying to make other people see things your way or do what you think is right. It is hard enough to manage ourselves, and much more to control others. Focus instead on asking "What else can I do?" and "What can I change about myself?" You can also avoid compounding your suffering by surrendering to that which God allows. Submit yourself to God, accept His will, whatever it may be, and enjoy the peace it bestows. You take care of your own business, let others take care of theirs, and let God be God and do what He wills.

I approach the game of tennis in an analogous way. When playing singles, I realize I cannot control the game's outcome. Only one person can win, and God already knows who, regardless of how much I beg. I also cannot dictate how my opponent should play, or his attitude on the court. Hence, I prepare for each match by setting goals of things I can control, and then do all I can to meet them. I determine how I am going to play and what specific techniques I would focus on executing well during the match; the only elements over which I have control. When playing doubles, a team sport concept, I focus only on how I play. I cannot dictate how well my partner plays or how much effort he exerts; I can only determine mine. All I can do is encourage and support him. If I were to focus on worrying about how my partner plays, I would end up distracted; this could be detrimental to my own performance. All I can control is how I play and what attitude I choose to have during the match.

Even if it takes three to tango, we are assigned only our own part. That is a comforting thought. Why worry about our partner's or God's part when we cannot control them? Sometimes, it is a struggle even to keep up with our own. We just need to keep dancing our part as if that is all it takes and that is all that matters. Maybe, not worrying about the irrelevant is what will give us the peace we seek.

"Although it takes three to tango, you can control only one. You cannot change the thoughts or behaviors of another, and you cannot control God; you can only control and change yourself."

Part II: Seeking Contentment

Dear God,

Sometimes, I want things to be the way I want them.

I'm not satisfied with what You've given me.

Help me trust You that all I have is all I need.

Give me a grateful heart and quench my desire for more.

CHAPTER 5
TAKING LIFE AS IS

Sometimes, we resist life and say, "*This is not how things should be.*" Instead of accepting what it brings, we want life to unfold according to how we think it should. Some of us believe we all should go to college, get married, have children, and get a high-paying job, even if these paths do not match our priorities. Even when we are slowed down by aging or sidelined by declining health, we sometimes insist that we should continue to function like we always had. Towards some of our friends, we expect them to act and think like us, even when they have different personalities and backgrounds. Some of us obsess about looking like the person we see on television, even if we do not have the same genetic makeup. We often set unrealistic expectations based on an arbitrary standard that our fragile minds concocted. Consequently, our world falls apart, and we become disheartened when we fail to meet them.

We should live life consciously and proactively but make allowance for it to amaze us by passively letting life play out according to its divine purpose. It is like planting a seed. We till the soil before sowing the seed, then fertilize and water it regularly. In the meantime, we sit back, and wait patiently and expectantly. Not all seeds will germinate, and those that do will grow into different unique shapes and sizes despite what we do. It would be futile to insist on our own design, so it is better not to.

Life is beautiful as is, and we should appreciate it at face value. Even the scars we wear tell a story of a life fully lived and reveal the strength of our character that helped us heal and survive. The blend of joyous celebrations and sorrowful afflictions made us more complete and become better versions of ourselves. We came into this world empty-handed. Hence, we are not entitled to anything. All we have acquired and experienced were gifts from God. No one should demand from the giver what the gifts should be. We are to enjoy our journey and be grateful for everything we were given. We can aspire and inspire change where needed, but we should not force it to happen our way. Whatever the circumstances, we should make the most of what we have, find beauty in every gift, and learn all the lessons that can be learned.

Having meaningful relationships in life contributes to our overall happiness. Our family and close friends support us, give us a sense of belonging, and allow us to experience genuine love. They are precious gifts from God, but no one can be everything to us. They are also as imperfect as we are. Hence, we are to accept them for who they are, enjoy the unique love that each one gives, and recognize that they can only give what they have. We should be grateful for whatever they can share and not resent what they cannot. We should enjoy them as they are and not lose our joy waiting for them to become what we think they should be. The same principle applies to our relationship with ourselves. We are to accept ourselves the way we are and love our uniqueness. We need to learn to love ourselves and others not only because of the qualities we possess but, more importantly, despite what we are or what we lack. Making mistakes is an integral part of our growth. We should be patient and give each other time to learn and mature. In the meantime, we need to adjust our expectations. No one should recognize a flaw in himself and ignore it. We should influence and inspire people close to us to change when needed and seek to do the same for ourselves, but not wait until we become perfect before we learn to appreciate the good in us and others. Do not set a bar by which we reject ourselves and others when we do not reach it. If there is any good in someone, we should keep them, value them, and not write them off and squander a precious gift God has given us.

Life is always evolving. Change ceases when life does. To receive life as it is means to accept that change is inevitable. Resisting this by insisting on what life should be will only lead to frustration and unhappiness. We need to always accept what is true and real now. It is futile to live in the past, dwell on regrets, and wonder what could have been. It is equally pointless to live in the future and drown in anxiety wondering which outcome life will take you. It is more fruitful to accept whatever situation we are in, make no judgment about it, adapt as best as we can, and make the most of the gift of life we were given. Seeking to make the most of every moment can be, in and of itself, one's purpose in life. Focusing on this could help us cope with the negative impact of some changes we encounter. Life does not have to be perfect for us to be happy. We can always find a reason to be happy if we want to; some are obvious, while others require eyes that are willing to see. Acknowledging that the world owes us nothing makes it easier to be grateful for the little things we have in our possession. A willingness to see God's fingerprints in every circumstance, even in the most insignificant ones, would leave us in awe of God's love and remind us of His constant presence around us. This gives us a sense of security, comfort, and peace. Despite the challenges or lack, being grateful for life as is helps us enjoy living and be truly happy.

I am generally happy and content with my life. I have learned to enjoy life as it is, relishing the sweet things and accepting the bitter and spicy ones that add vibrance to it. Together, they turned my life from good to great. A life without suffering will leave me shallow and insensitive. A life without discomfort and difficulties will leave me weak and unprepared for challenges I may face. I do not like to suffer, and neither would anyone, but I accept it as a necessary tool to deepen my experience of life and my relationship with God. Everything will eventually break, and I accept that. In the meantime, I will enjoy what I have now and focus on gaining wisdom, courage, strength, and patience from difficult life situations; they will help me take on future challenges. I am very thankful I have people to love, and I got to experience other people's love. No one person could give me all I need every time I need them. But God gave me a loving family and many loyal friends, who gave me what they could, and collectively, my needs were always met. I dream big, but I do not reach them all. There is not enough time anyway to achieve them all, nor do I need all that I wish for. I am very content with what I have because God has always blessed me with more than I needed and more than I deserved. Life is great as is. I trust God to design and manage it. All there is for me to do is accept and enjoy it; that is not a bad deal.

CHAPTER 6
LESS OF ME

What would life be like if we used "I" less often? "I am," "I want," "I will," "I like," and "I should." What would our lives be like if we spent less time planning our next big vacation? Less time thinking of the next big toy purchase? Less time defending ourselves? Less time proving that we are better? Less time worrying about the future and regretting the past? Less time being angry? Less time complaining? Less time correcting others? Less time trying to avoid discomfort and inconvenience? Less time seeking pleasure? Less time insisting others love us? If we spend less time thinking of ourselves, we may have more time to think of others. If we spend less time seeking our own happiness, we might actually end up finding it.

In John 12: 24, Jesus said, *"Unless a kernel of wheat falls to the ground and dies, it remains only a single seed. But if it dies, it produces many seeds."* One of life's most significant contradictions is that we must deny ourselves to find happiness. So many rich and famous people are constantly seeking more, using their wealth and influence to find happiness. Despite this, it continues to elude them. Jim Carrey, an American comedian and actor, was succinct when he said, *"I think everybody should get rich and famous and do everything they ever dreamed of so they can see that it's not the answer."* Many of us are fixated on looking out for our self-interests in the act of self-preservation and promotion, only to find ourselves chasing our tails. We are thirsty, but we look for the kind of water that does not quench our thirst. We continue to yearn for satisfaction, but our eyes are directed inwards, and we miss the mark.

Imagine being by the lake and focused on your reflection in the still water. You were so concerned about how you looked that you did not get to appreciate the beauty of the trees, the warmth of the sun, and the cool breeze. The image on the water is a mere reflection; it is not reality. It cannot give us joy, and it will not satisfy us. We need to look beyond ourselves and admire the splendor that surrounds us. We need to let God's creations amaze us and teach us to keep giving without asking for anything in return. If our goal in life is to delight ourselves with all the worldly pleasures we can obtain, chase accolades, and make known to everyone we are always right, we will constantly long for more. Preoccupation with ourselves and gratification of our desires without regard for others is like craving ice cream. After we finish eating the first cone, we want another one. We are thrilled to get the second one, even though we do not need it. We eat it anyway, only to feel sick because we had too much and end up more dissatisfied than before we began. We attain true contentment when we put the needs of others before our own. Being self-centered does not satisfy, but we continue doing it, hoping one day it will. Unfortunately, the more we indulge in this behavior, the unhappier we become.

If we choose not to do what our natural self is inclined to do because it is not right, that is self-control. If we give away what we have when there is only enough for ourselves, that is self-sacrifice. If we allow others to think they won the argument, even if we believe otherwise, that is magnanimity. If we do not seek recognition for our good works, need a reason to apologize, or require justification to overlook someone's fault, that is humility. If we put aside our concerns about our own problems and forget our comfort as we seek to help others, that is self-denial. We live in a culture where many ask, *"What's in it for me?"* It is the *quid pro quo* ethos. Because of this, people are skeptical of others' good deeds. In fact, an often-repeated advice by some is to presume that everyone is looking out only for their own interests. We must submit ourselves to God and let our old selves die; the self that thinks too much of himself and believes that his needs are above everybody else's. As we have more of God's nature, there will be less of ourselves manifesting in our thoughts, words, and actions. As a result, self-control, self-sacrifice, kindness, humility, and self-denial become second nature to us. To die to self is the path to peace, contentment, satisfaction, and happiness.

The people who are genuinely happy and content with their lives have mastered themselves. They have learned to control their tendencies and can deny the beckoning of their flesh at will. The world no longer holds them hostage because they are detached from it. These people are truly free. Even when others falsely malign them, they see no need to defend themselves. The confidence their conscience gives them negates the need to seek the approval of others. Even when no one gives them recognition or praise, they see no need to prop themselves up or prove they are better than the rest. They have accepted themselves for who they are and are happy with their lives. Besides, there will always be someone better or less than them, and they are wise enough not to compare. The lure of the material world does not appeal to them. They recognize that nothing in this world lasts, and everything eventually breaks. Indulging in worldly possessions and desires feeds the body and does nothing for the spirit. The flesh is fickle and continues to decay daily. What is sufficient or fulfilling today may not be the same tomorrow. The threshold to satisfy keeps increasing. We develop tolerance and require continuous escalation of the stimulus to satisfy. So, why even chase it? They have also learned the futility of seeking to control others and letting others' behavior bother them; their focus is on improving themselves. These enlightened people do not need the world to bow to them. They forgive whenever it is called for and live in peace with others. They do not insist that others love them. Their happiness is not controlled by what others give or withhold. They gladly accept what is provided to them and demand nothing. Those who live a life of self-denial learn to face suffering with calmness. They know that life is not meant to be a bed of roses and find value in the lessons that suffering teaches. It is all about improving themselves and not simply pleasing. Furthermore, they are detached from the past and the future. There is so much they are called to do in the present that they do not have time to give in to the temptation of self-pity and worry. Mastery of self can save us from unnecessary pain and suffering when we can avoid giving in to those desires that we know lead to destruction. To be selfless is to think of ourselves less. It is being less concerned over how we feel, what we desire, or what we need. To achieve this, we need to be motivated by something higher than ourselves and one that has eternal value; pleasing God is the strongest motivation to become other-centered. It takes practice to develop the right habits to help us get there. Since we become like the one with whom we spend the most time, I believe this ambitious and formidable goal can be achieved by spending more time with God in prayer and meditation and knowing Him better through reading the scriptures. Repetition and consistency are key. We need to make up our minds and commit to it. By committing, we recognize at the outset that this will not be easy and there will be ups and downs, but we are going to keep running this race until the finish line.

This world will continue to exist without us. We are not the reason the world came to be. We are not entitled to anything. Life is not all about us. The purpose of our existence is not to live for ourselves, but to honor God by serving others. St. Augustine said, *"You have made us for yourself, Oh Lord, and our hearts are restless until they rest in you."* We need to starve our ego and awaken to the awareness that selfishness does not satisfy. We need to look beyond ourselves to find true happiness.

"*If we spend less time seeking our own happiness, we might actually end up finding it.*"

CHAPTER 7
EITHER WAY, I'M OKAY

"… I have learned to be content whatever the circumstances. I know what it is to be in need, and I know what it is to have plenty. I have learned the secret of being content in any and every situation, whether well fed or hungry, whether living in plenty or in want. I can do all this through Him who gives me strength … and my God will meet all your needs according to the riches of his glory in Christ Jesus." Philippians 4:11-13, 19.

S
ome of us are inclined to believe our success was achieved because of our hard work alone. This drives us to keep pushing ourselves, sometimes beyond our limits, because we take sole responsibility for the outcome. On the surface, this sounds awe-inspiring until we see the despair and discontent experienced when expectations are not met. Our sense of self-sufficiency and self-reliance leads to self-blame when we fail to acknowledge there are events and circumstances we cannot control. During a time when we need to be our loudest cheerleaders, we become our worst critics instead. How we define success can also affect how we deal with disappointments. When our success depends on other people's failure or achieving superiority over others, we will never be content. We will be pleased with ourselves until we discover others have achieved more. In our mind, a new standard has been set. Hence, we push ourselves to work even harder hoping to meet or exceed it. We skip lunch, stay at the office longer, and give up sleep. Most likely, this new approach will eventually produce

the result we hope for and make us happy, until we learn that someone outperformed us again. Consequently, we strive for more and more because what we achieved is no longer adequate. We are never content because our primary motivation for the things we do is to be better than everyone else.

Our ego can drive us off the cliff as we strive to succeed in life, and it can also push us deeper into hopelessness and isolation when we fail. In times of sorrow and lack, many of us try to remain strong, stay focused, and channel all our energies into attempting to remedy our situation. We seem to cope well until the problem persists longer than expected; we continue to give it our all hoping to overcome. We sometimes erroneously believe it was our own doing that got us into a bind. Therefore, it is our sole responsibility to get us out of it. We decline to accept help offered by the people around us who love us. As mental and physical fatigue set in, our will to fight declines. Self-pity, despair, and worry start to overwhelm us. This leads us to seek out destructive vices and fleeting pleasures to provide distraction and relief, even for just a moment. With time, the amount we require to dull our pain continues to increase until we become prisoners of the very things we hope will set us free. Ironically, our attempt at self-sufficiency drains our energy reserves and leaves us helpless.

We are prone to discontent both during times of abundance and scarcity, if we rely on our ego to direct what we do and how we live. Some people are never content and constantly want more because they derive satisfaction in being better than everyone else around them. The truth is, whenever we look around, there will always be somebody better than us. It is also delusional to believe that in everything, we can get the results we desire if we put our hearts and minds into it. This often leads to disappointment due to factors we cannot control that derail our plans. It is good to be strong and resilient in the face of challenges, but it is vanity to think we can do it all ourselves. This false sense of adequacy can also lead to discouragement. To remain balanced and content always, we have to acknowledge that all we have, the good and the bad, are gifts from God. He alone decides what to give and the conditions, limitations, and durations of the gifts; we are not entitled to any of them. It is for us to decide whether we will enjoy what we were given or wait until we get what we want before we do. We must also discern the meaning and purpose of our feeling of lack. Because all we have are from God, they will give us joy only if we use them for the reasons He intended. It is comforting for us to recognize that the giver knows what and how much we need, and He will always be there to lend a hand when we need it. Having humility and faith will spare us disillusionment when things do not go our way. In whatever we do, if we pursue them with a clear objective of obeying the will of the giver and trying to accomplish His intentions, we should not worry about the outcome for it is His concern. Given God's personal stake in all this, would He not encourage, direct, strengthen, and enlighten us when we need them? When our ego leads us to ask, "*Why me?*" amid suffering and difficulties, we should remind ourselves that it is an honor to be chosen by God to serve Him. I believe God would only choose someone He thinks is capable and worthy.

All I have was given to me by God; they are gifts. Yes, I worked hard for all of them, but if God had not blessed my efforts, all the arduous work would have been for naught. Many things in my life also happened because I was at the right place and time. How can I claim then that my successes came from my own efforts? The result might not have been the same if my circumstances had been slightly different. I was given more than I deserved. How can I ask for more? I also could not, in conscience, take all the gifts and use them for my own pleasure and self-promotion. I know for sure that God gave me what I have because He wants me to use them to serve others. I am a mere steward of the many gifts I received. My job is to share and deliver them according to God's plans. I am content with what I have, but that does not mean I do not seek to continue improving myself and striving for more. I will maximize the use of my talents, pursue my passions, and aim to become what God intended for me to be. I shall do all these knowing that beneath the worldly pursuits is a desire to use what I have attained to serve others and be the answer to their prayers. Hopefully, how I pursue my dreams will meet God's approval, regardless of whether man approves. This perspective on life is what will lead to contentment.

It is hard to be content when life is not going our way. No one wants to be hurt, lonely, or poor. Furthermore, no one wants to suffer perpetually. However, it is possible to be at peace despite the pain if we try to see things from God's perspective. Suffering becomes more bearable if we face them with a sense of purpose, knowing that God willed it for our good, protection, sanctification, or growth. Going through challenging times can undoubtedly make us wiser and stronger. It can even repair what is broken, prepare us to help and serve others, lead us to people who need us, and inspire others to follow us. We need to submit to God's will and rest in His assurance that He will always be by our side, fight our battles, comfort, and heal us. Even if we do not know what to do, He does. Even if we cannot fix or change the situation, He can. Even if we do not have the strength to fight, He does.

When our world is falling apart, we should seek the presence of God and enjoy the peace His presence gives. Remember that God is close to the brokenhearted. We will find Him when we seek Him. Our pains and fears naturally draw us closer to Him. If we remain in His presence, we will experience the peace He promised. We hear His kind and loving voice that tells us, *"It will be okay."* As we rest, He is making things happen. He is changing hearts, fixing what is broken, breaking chains of addiction, giving sight to those who cannot see the light, getting the attention of those who would not listen, healing broken hearts and troubled relationships, satisfying those who are longing to be loved, restoring health, and granting peace.

Everything eventually breaks, and people come and go. We should be grateful for the time we had them and not waste a moment dwelling on what we lost; be hopeful for better things that are coming our way. Avoid looking too close at problems and missing the big picture. Step back a little and let God show us what He sees from His vantage point. In the meantime, we should trust our all-knowing and all-powerful God that He knows what He is doing and has the power to change or fix everything. We can rest assured in knowing that He is always with us wherever in life we may be. Whatever the outcome of our present struggles, we have confidence that all will be well. This is faith, and faith is the secret to being content, whether life brings you sunshine or brings you rain.

"It is possible to be at peace despite the pain if we try to see things from God's perspective."

Part III: Seeking Encouragement

Dear God,

The unrelenting challenges I face wear me down.

Lend me Your hand

and help me make it through another day.

Give me hope to find the strength to take another step.

CHAPTER 8
TREASURES IN TRIBULATIONS

E very challenging situation we face is an opportunity for growth. During the Covid pandemic, we were forced to put on hold life as we know it. Businesses had to change their usual practices. Consequently, many of us discovered better ways of doing things and found a passion for activities we never imagined. During the Great Recession from 2007 to 2009, the value of stocks dropped precipitously and continued over an extended period, and there was no indication of the bottom. I, like many others, withdrew my investments for fear of losing them all. Those more experienced in this kept their investments intact and weathered the storm. Some even bought more stocks of great companies as they were trading at better prices. They saw an opportunity, while many like me saw catastrophe. Over time, the world economy recovered and corrected itself, and as expected based on historical data, stock values rose exponentially following the crash.

Life is a long-term investment. We are not here to seek transient pleasures and fleeting worldly gains. Instead, we allow ourselves to be chiseled by the trials of daily life until we take a form that reflects the image of God. Like stocks, short-term failures and life's disappointments are not predictive of long-term success. The frequency of our ups and downs in life creates a sawtooth pattern. For as long as the line on the graph keeps trending upward, we should be good in the grander scheme of things. In the book of James 1:2-4, he wrote, *"Consider it pure joy, my brothers and sisters, whenever you face trials of many kinds, because you know that the testing of your faith produces perseverance. Let perseverance finish its work so that you may be mature and complete, not lacking anything."* A life crisis can compel us to learn better ways to live. Sometimes, that is what it takes to soften our hearts and open our minds to accept correction. However, when trials become painful, we sometimes withdraw from God and soothe our pain by returning to sin, only to realize this worsens the pain. We eventually learn that when we are in pain, we are better off to hold on to God, rest in His love, and anticipate deepening our trust and faith in Him. This eventually leads to true peace and happiness. If we keep our eyes on our goal, we will continue to rise after a fall. The lessons we learn from each fall push us forward and upward faster toward our objective. As we achieve a certain level of maturity in our faith, we become capable of going outside our comfort zone. Instead of focusing on our own growth, we now find meaning and satisfaction in reaching out to others and doing great things to honor God through serving others.

When faced with setbacks, challenges, or unfavorable circumstances that disturb the status quo, it is important to acknowledge and view their existence without judgment. We should avoid labeling them as bad, difficult, stressful, disappointing, or painful. Our focus should be on figuring out what we can do given the reality we face. Resisting reality is a waste of time. We should channel our energy towards making the best use of what we have, contemplate how we can turn a negative situation into something favorable, and seek out new opportunities that these impediments have compelled us to consider. Living in self-pity, asking why things had to happen this way, is a fruitless exercise. We have no power to alter the course of something that has already happened. There are also some things over which we have no control. Pondering why something happened should be limited to discerning what lessons we can learn from it.

In the book "*Tuesdays with Morrie*," author Mitch Albom chronicled the time he spent with his mentor Morrie Schwartz during the last few months of his life. He shared with us the lessons he learned from a dying man about how to live. This book was translated into 48 languages and sold nearly 18 million copies worldwide. Even at the brink of death, Morrie made beneficial use of his time here on earth and inspired and encouraged millions. Jan Koum and Brian Acton co-developed WhatsApp, a popular instant messaging application. They were both rejected by Facebook when they applied for a job in 2009, only to sell WhatsApp to Facebook in 2014 for $19.3 billion. On August 4, 2009, Acton tweeted, "*Facebook turned me down. It was a great opportunity to connect with some fantastic people. Looking forward to life's next adventure.*" They did not get the job, but they built relationships and made connections during the application process. This great rejection led to the largest acquisition to date at the time.

When our lives were turned upside down during the Covid pandemic, we all had to adapt to survive. People were getting sick and unable to work. We were forced to isolate and keep our distance from others to avoid getting and making others sick. As a result, our economy tanked. Businesses needed to find ways to continue their operations to keep the lights on. People were asked to work from home. Meetings were held remotely via video applications. Restaurants were closed for in-room dining but they tried to keep the cash flowing with take-out and delivery orders. As grim as the situation was, the pandemic eventually ended. However, the new way of doing business we adopted remained. It became apparent that allowing employees to work from home was desirable for them and beneficial for companies as it lowered overhead costs. Video applications like Zoom, Teams, and FaceTime flourished as online meetings became standard practice even after the pandemic. It was convenient, and it reduced travel expenses. Food delivery services like Uber Eats, Door Dash, and Grubhub have become new cultural phenomenon and are likely here to stay. Consumers realized the convenience of having food delivered to their homes, and restaurants that did not have the resources to have their own delivery service, can now do so in a more cost-effective method. Stock prices dropped during the economic downturn. The economic outlook was grim, but to some, it was an opportunity to buy stocks in good companies at a lower cost. The crisis that was Covid led to changes that improved our lives. Thanks to those people who faced what was meant to destroy us and turned it into something positive. They recognized new opportunities born out of this tragedy and did what they could to cope. Many not only survived but they thrived in the face of enormous difficulties.

As the earth unceasingly revolves around the sun, our lives also do not cease to evolve. Our bodies continue to age, and we lose certain abilities in the process. Likewise, the wear and tear of daily living contribute to our inability to maintain the status quo. Similarly, people in our lives come and go. We encounter them along the way in life's journey; some stay for a minute, and only a few are with us for a lifetime. Although our physical prowess diminishes over time, our wisdom and maturity increase. A basketball player may not be able to jump as high when he ages, but his knowledge of the game deepens. It is wise to see this coming and accept it. The player can then transition to helping others as a coach or trainer and continue contributing to the game he loves. When we suffer injuries or succumb to illness, it is wise to acknowledge our disability, keep our minds busy, and our days productive by focusing on parts of our body that remain intact. For as long as we are alive, we must live with a sense of purpose. Do not fret about what we lost but be grateful for what we still have and use them to serve God by serving others. It is in helping others that we find meaning in life. When people we love leave us for whatever reason or lose appreciation for us with or without cause, it is wise to accept that this is not within our power to control. Recognize that we only have so much time and energy to spare in a day. Loving someone takes time and energy. Understand that because someone left, there is now room to welcome someone else. There are always people out there who need somebody and would appreciate what we have to offer.

God never promised us a life without suffering or difficulties. In fact, Jesus said in Luke 14: 27, *"And whoever does not carry their cross and follow me cannot be my disciple."* Trials and tribulations mold us, sanctify us, and strengthen us. We are encouraged to welcome them. In Romans 5: 3-4, St. Paul said, *"… we also glory in our sufferings, because we know that suffering produces perseverance; perseverance, character; and character, hope."* There is value in struggles and dealing with challenges. Suffering builds our character and prepares us to do remarkable things. In 2 Corinthians 4: 16-17, St. Paul also said, *"Therefore we do not lose heart. Though outwardly we are wasting away, yet inwardly we are being renewed day by day. For our light and momentary troubles are achieving for us an eternal glory that far outweighs them all."* In my first book, *Divine Intervention: A Story of Healing, Love, and Hope*, I shared the pain and suffering my family and I went through as we faced the life-threatening illness of our youngest daughter. Even though I would not want to go through this again and would not wish it on anyone, I am very thankful for what that experience has done for my family and me. I would not have the passion and energy for the work I do now encouraging and inspiring others, if it were not for the baptism of fire I received. Even though God allows suffering in our lives to achieve His divine purpose, He promised to help us through it. In Isaiah 43:2, He said, *"When you pass through the waters, I will be with you; and when you pass through the rivers, they will not sweep over you. When you walk through the fire, you will not be burned; the flames will not set you ablaze."* Welcome challenges and difficulties in life as if they are our friends who are there to give us tough love. We need to view them not as problems but as opportunities to help elevate us to the next level.

"*Every challenging situation we face is an opportunity for growth.*"

CHAPTER 9
CONQUERING OUR MOUNTAIN

Recently, I met up with a friend I had not seen for almost 20 years. It was nice to catch up and share how our lives had evolved since we last saw each other. We reviewed the lessons we learned, celebrated our successes, and encouraged each other for challenges we still face. As we parted, he left me pondering about a statement he made. He said, *"I understand it intellectually, but I pray that I can see it as clearly as you do one day. Maybe then, I can get out of my chrysalis and become a beacon of hope to others."*

Challenges in life can be daunting when we look at the formidable path laid out in front of us or when there is a thick fog that blinds us to what is ahead. The daily battles that impede our advancement to the finish line can be exhausting. Often, it is the persistent seemingly minor nuisance that causes us to quit or fail. *"Catch for us the foxes, the little foxes that ruin the vineyards, our vineyards that are in bloom* (Song of Songs 2:15)." There is no one solution that fixes everything, and there is not one philosophy that will address all things. Life is very complex, we are all unique, and situations are highly variable. We need different tools in our toolbox to remove the different nails and screws that keep us bound where we are.

Accept and let go. Sometimes we sleepwalk through life; we simply exist. We sleep, wake up, eat, go back to sleep, and repeat. We are blind and numb to what is going on around us. Sometimes, it is because we are so intensely focused on what we want, what we think life should be, how bad we feel, regrets about past mistakes, and anxiety about how little of life is left. Now and then, we get a fleeting moment of awareness and realize time has gone by and we have not really lived. To feel alive, we must accept life as it is. We must accept everything and everyone it brings, acknowledge that what has already happened cannot be undone, and take every experience and person as is. The alternative is to resist life and ignore reality, which does not change regardless of our decision whether to acknowledge them. Because we are not busy trying to stop reality from happening, our minds are calm and not exhausted. Hence, we have the strength and time to tackle life's challenges and have the fortitude to determine what we can and need to fix and what we cannot and need to let go. Holding on to hurts, frustrations, regrets, and anger is hoarding unwanted and unneeded baggage that only weighs us down and keeps us from moving forward. The quicker we can accept reality, the sooner we can decide what to let go. The better we are at letting go, the freer we feel. We then achieve this state of being okay even if life from the outside does not seem to be.

Be grateful. It would be nonsensical, and even outright hypocritical, to tell someone that they should be grateful when their loved one just died, their marriage failed, they fell ill, or their friend betrayed them. In 1 Thessalonians 5:18, St. Paul encouraged us to *"give thanks in all circumstances."* It may be hard to give thanks *for* all circumstances, especially when they are negative. Still, it is possible to be grateful *in* all circumstances, whether easy or difficult. Being grateful is a state of mind and spirit. It cannot be achieved by forcing ourselves to mechanically come up with a list of things to be thankful for, especially in times of despair and depression. During those bleak and gloomy moments, we would not have the energy to think. The objective is not to suppress negative emotions but to elevate our hearts and minds into the realm of faith. In this zone, there is calm and hope in the awareness that we are loved by God, whom we can depend on to protect, care for, teach, encourage, and strengthen us. Even if all that we come to know in this world were to leave us, God's love for us remains consistent and permanent. It is this assurance that gives us a reason to be grateful despite our dire circumstances. In our grief, God will show us the depth of our love for someone, and how blessed we are to have had someone to love and be loved equally in return. He will allow us to experience the profundity of the comfort He gives. In our failure and despair, God will reveal our dependence on Him. He will heal our toxic pride, grow our character, and lead us to a life of humility. How else can we learn that? In our loneliness, we experience intimacy with God that no human relationship can give. In the pain of abandonment and neglect, we come to know that God never leaves us, even when we turn our backs on Him when it is inconvenient to remain faithful. In sickness, God allows us to learn how to trust Him alone. In frustration, He teaches us patience when all other means He tried failed. In allowing us to experience regret and shame for our past mistakes, God helps make it easier for us to overlook the faults of others and forgive them. And when God still loves us when no one would, we learn to forgive ourselves. We reckon that it does not matter what the world thinks of us or what we think of ourselves. All that matters is that it does not matter to God how badly we have fallen. In all these sufferings, we gain wisdom and develop a grateful heart. We learn to be thankful for what we once had, even if they are now reduced to but a memory. We are thankful for what we still have and everything we continue to receive. Being alive in and of itself is more than enough reason to be thankful. Even if we were to lose everything and everyone in our lives, we are thankful for the assurance that we will never be without the love of God. "*Neither death nor life, neither angels nor demons, neither the present nor the future, nor any powers, neither height nor depth, nor anything else in all creation, will be able to separate us from the love of God* (Romans 8:38-39)." As our gratitude overflows for the blessings we received, especially if we did nothing to deserve them, we naturally become generous to others. It is difficult to be grateful and generous and be negative at the same time. Hence, inner peace and joy eventually follow regardless of our circumstances. To achieve this state of gratefulness, we must live consciously and be fully mindful of every moment. In this condition of focused awareness, we experience reality, including the presence of God who is always with us. We experience His love with every breath we take, even with tears trickling down our cheeks. Our eyes start to see the extraordinary in the ordinary, and we witness miracles where once there was no hope on the horizon. Each experience brings us closer to the summit of our mountain.

Eyes on the ball. In tennis, I was trained to keep my eyes on the ball. When the opponent hits it, I do not have time to pause and analyze where the ball might go during the fast-paced action. I cannot stand around and just pray for God to direct the ball where I want it to go. I cannot afford to dwell on the last shot I hit lest I miss the next ball coming my way. I cannot worry about how the opponent will play and what kind of ball he will send me. All I can do is keep my eyes on the ball every time it is live and bouncing on the court. I must say that life imitates sports. When trying to climb the mountains we face in life, we need to focus on putting one foot in front of the other. We cannot be overly concerned about getting to the summit when we still have a thousand miles to cross. We must be fully present in the moment we face. There is no time to argue about how things should be or try to manipulate them to become what we want them to be. We simply need to do what is necessary given the circumstances at hand. It is unwise to sit back and worry about what might happen or insist that God changes His will to suit ours. We can only control ourselves and change what is in the present. Hence, we should focus on the here and now. Always accept and pay full attention to what is currently happening. The past is a distraction, and the future is but a fantasy. Take one step and then the next. If we can take one more, there is no reason to stop.

Pray and meditate. Like my friend, we often understand intellectually what we need to do to conquer our mountain. However, to reach the point of enlightenment where we truly understand and conduct our lives accordingly in a consistent way, we need time and practice. We need to develop a habit and lifestyle of prayer and meditation to achieve that goal. Prayer increases our awareness of God's constant presence, and meditation enhances our understanding of ourselves in relation to the world surrounding us and the things happening to us. Walking in God's presence helps us make the right choices and gives us the courage to withstand difficulties. Understanding there are many things in life we cannot control which will happen regardless of our wishes teaches us to accept things as they are and live in harmony with the world. There is no pinnacle of enlightenment, as we will quickly realize we are not fully enlightened the moment we think we are. Life on Earth will always have its peaks and valleys. We will succeed in one thing and soon after, fail in another. There will always be something along the way that will challenge us and push us to keep going higher. We can rely on prayer to help us find the strength to endure, and practice meditation to make us aware when our minds wander off to a place that discourages us. They keep us calm, motivate us to repent, and circle back to our original intention.

Sir Edmund Hillary said, *"It is not the mountains that we conquer, but ourselves."* We created the mountains we are trying to conquer. Mountains are made from our flaws, imperfections, wounds, and scars. We can stand at the base and gaze at it with dismay. We can also blame others for putting us in this predicament and settle in complacency thinking it was not our fault. Or we can take the first of many thousand steps and keep going one step at a time, learning, growing, changing what we can, and making amends as we go. We trip, slide, and fall along the way, but we keep getting up and pushing ourselves forward with the help of God and the people He sends our way. Our goal is not to wish our problems away, but rather, to conquer ourselves so we do not create the same mountain for us to climb again. When we get to the summit, our view of the world will be broader and much clearer. Hopefully, with this new vision, my friend, we can truly be a beacon of hope for others.

Chapter 10
New Beginnings, New Endings

"The steadfast love of the Lord never ceases; His mercies never come to an end; they are new every morning; great is your faithfulness. "The Lord is my portion," says my soul, "therefore I will hope in Him." Lamentations 3:22-24.

There is a sense of finality about the past. Once a moment passes, we can never bring it back. Some people dwell on the past and live in regret and shame. They live in a world constructed in their minds out of scraps from memories of mistakes and failures, where all they can do is think about what could have been or what they should have done. In this self-manufactured world, nothing changes because nothing can be done. As a result, its inhabitants drown in depression and hopelessness riding on this rocking chair they hope will take them to a better place.

But we all have a choice. We can live in the past and be depressed or get busy living in the present and be hopeful. For as long as we are alive, there is always an opportunity for a new beginning. When a relationship fails, you can repair it and start anew, or build a new one altogether. If you have not been a good parent for the past twenty years, you can try being a better one for the next twenty; it's never too late. If you went with the wrong crowd and got involved with drugs and alcohol and did poorly in high school, you have another chance to do well in college and hope for a better future. If you run your business to the ground because of poor judgment or lost your job because of shoddy work ethics, there are always new opportunities to apply what you learned from your mistakes and be successful next time. If you sinned against God, in small or big ways, once or repeatedly, you could repent and know for sure that God will forgive you.

No matter how grave our mistakes or how deep a hole we dug for ourselves, there is always hope. Each new day brings hope for a new beginning. We want a reset and an opportunity to start over, and we hope we get it right this time. But what we are really hoping for is not just a new beginning but rather a new and better ending. We want another chance to approach life differently in a way that leads to an end where we feel fulfilled, at peace, and truly happy. Unless we can clearly identify the specific outcome or ending we desire, each opportunity for a new beginning will be a journey to nowhere. We would continue to live a life of new beginnings without attaining the new endings we hoped for.

Everyone deserves a second chance. We all made mistakes in our lives and will continue to make mistakes for the rest of our lives. Just as we are not infallible, the people around us are not either. It is important to learn to forgive yourself and forgive others always. We should be magnanimous in forgiving and humble in receiving forgiveness. Life is a race. Some know where the finish line is, but some are lost. Some will falter along the way, and some will quit altogether. We are all in this race together; no one benefits when one of us does not finish the race. Let us encourage each other along the way by helping those who fall to rise and continue running. Remind them that every day is a new day and a chance to pursue a new beginning. When it is up to you to decide, always give yourself and others a second chance. It does not matter how many times we have to start over. What matters is our willingness to try again. We do not stop trying just because we keep making the same mistake; in the same way, we do not quit eating just because we get hungry again a few hours after we eat. Because life is a race, we need the discipline to train, practice, and regulate what we consume. We need to make time for prayer and the study of God's word. We need to practice living the way we want to live. We need to be around people who will help us grow spiritually, and we must be selective in what we choose to watch, listen to, and talk about. Maya Angelou, a famous American poet and civil rights activist, once said, *"Do the best you can until you know better. Then when you know better, do better."* Yes, we all deserve a second chance, but it is up to us whether we choose to take it.

Repeating the same action that led to an undesirable outcome will yield the same result. When presented with an opportunity to start anew, we should apply the lessons we learned from our mistakes and try a different approach. The hope of having a new and better ending begins by accepting the gift of a new beginning.

Chapter 11
Growth in Giving No Excuses

When dealing with daily challenges in life, our minds tend to view ourselves as the victim, and circumstances and others as the cause of our misfortune. This faulty thinking is egotistical as it is "all about me." Without basis, we assume that we are not supposed to suffer; if we do, it is the fault of external forces. It is as if the world was made for us, and our happiness is the responsibility of others. Instead of correcting our mistakes and dealing with our deficiencies, we waste our time and energy blaming others and trying to manipulate circumstances over which we have no control. Meanwhile, we neglect what ought to be done because we refuse to accept responsibility for our choices and the consequences that result from them.

In every dilemma we face, we are always given a choice. This is an inherent power that God gave us since the creation of Adam and Eve. Some choices are easier to make than others. The better choice is not always the easiest. Even if there are forces that try to sway us one way or the other, the ultimate decision rests in our hands. Therefore, whatever it is we end up choosing, it would be solely our own doing. The cigarette we picked up, put in our mouth, and lit was our decision. No one forced or coerced us. The big slice of chocolate cake we ate after a heavy meal, the forbidden relationship we entered, or the disadvantageous business deal we made because we were too complacent and did not adequately research our options, were decisions we made using our free will.

There is no question that numerous factors may affect our decision-making. We can blame it on addiction, stress, past experiences of lack, trauma or abuse, medical diagnosis, natural inclinations and tendencies, or intellectual deficiencies. Many of our excuses cannot be undone, avoided, changed, fixed, or forgotten. Those that can be corrected should be remedied promptly, and the rest should be acknowledged, accepted as quickly as possible for what they are, and managed earnestly. The sooner we can muster up the courage to take responsibility for our actions and the humility to accept their consequences, the better for us. There is healing and power in saying, *"I made a choice, it was a mistake, I have no one to blame, it was my fault, I take responsibility, and now it's time to make a change."* This declaration will allow us to accept the truth and give us the resilience to take corrective actions and make amends. It can save us from ruin and hopefully help us redeem ourselves.

Seeing a therapist, reading self-help books, and listening to inspirational talks are all useful resources and can help us overcome our struggles with human frailty. But listening and reading alone would not get us where we want to be. They tell us what we need to do and teach us how to do it, but they do not give us the power to accomplish our objectives. We often want to do the right thing but end up doing the opposite. Even St. Paul struggled with the same problem. He said in Romans 7:15, *"I do not understand what I do. For what I want to do I do not do, but what I hate I do."* Over the centuries, many philosophers and wise people have shared their wisdom with the world. I have indulged in their teachings and found them enlightening but undoubtedly insufficient in leading me to the life of peace and true happiness I yearn for. It was not until I got to know God and surrendered my will to His that I could fill the gaps these human teachers left and developed the confidence I needed to tackle future challenges that everyday life brings. In Isaiah 41:10, God said, *"So do not fear, for I am with you; do not be dismayed, for I am your God. I will strengthen you and help you; I will uphold you with my righteous right hand."* God gave me courage, wisdom, and power to make the right choices when I was weak and when my feelings tried to overtake my rational mind.

We have to guard against relying on our feelings to make decisions. In Jeremiah 17:9, it is said that *"The heart is deceitful above all things and beyond cure. Who can understand it?"* Our feelings are fickle and cannot always be trusted. It changes depending on the temperature of our circumstances. It also sometimes defies logic. Feelings can intoxicate us and make us forget or ignore the potential adverse consequences of certain actions. The tempter knows this and can use our feelings to distract us.

We must always be on guard and ready for this kind of spiritual battle; it is won or lost in our minds. Preparation is key. We need to fill our minds with thoughts that make it easy to choose what is right because it feels right. We also need to keep our minds in the present. Reviving emotions brought about by old hurts can tether us to a negative state of mind that could affect the choices we make today. Those past events that caused suffering are no longer reality. We experienced them and, hopefully, learned from them. Daydreaming and fantasizing about something we wish to happen in the future can be dangerous as well. Enticing ourselves to experience something that is yet to happen that we know could potentially hurt us is laying our own trap. Keeping our minds in the present seems like the safest place to operate. We need to submit ourselves to God and practice acting as He would like us to at every given opportunity to withstand the pull of intense emotions towards the dark side. In Galatians 5:16, St. Paul said, *"So I say, walk by the Spirit, and you will not gratify the desires of the flesh."* In Ephesians 6:11-17, he urged us to *"take up the shield of faith with which you can extinguish all the flaming arrows of the evil one,"* and the *"sword of the Spirit, which is the word of God."* Spending time with God in prayer and meditating on His teachings from the scriptures will help us build our spiritual stamina and prepare us for battle.

We seek to avoid doing what is wrong because we do not want to experience the pain, shame, sadness, and destruction from making poor choices. It is important to recognize the triggers that lead us to certain actions and be aware when they present themselves. An escape plan should be in place before there is a fire. When a crisis is in progress and the smoke clouds our judgment and makes it difficult to react appropriately, our immediate response should always be to take a deep breath and relax for a brief moment. We should recognize and accept what is actually happening, stay calm, assess the situation, and determine the solution. Fighting or denying reality distracts and directs our attention away from managing the crisis. We should take responsibility for what is ours, fix what we can, make amends if needed, and deal with the consequences. Let the pain and sorrow of the latter be our teacher and catalyst for change and growth, and not allow them to sink us deeper into the doldrums.

When we take responsibility for our own happiness, peace, health, and success, we are more likely to achieve them. We would suffer less and enjoy life more. We would not waste our energy trying to make others do what they cannot do or are unwilling to do. We would not depend on others and waste our time waiting for them to make things happen for us. We would not wait in futility for our circumstances to change or misuse our energy in manipulating reality to align with our wishes. Instead, we focus all our effort on managing how we respond to others and our situation and trying to better ourselves. Over time, we make better choices and get more desirable results. We will make mistakes, but if we take responsibility for our wrong choices and their consequences and learn from them, we will see growth and experience renewal. We should always do our best to make good choices but never let the fear of making mistakes stop us from living. There is no reason to live in shame and regret for mistakes made, as they are part of making us who we are today. Make the best decision based on what we know at the moment. If that turned out to be a wrong choice, we gained experience and wisdom if we let it teach us. For as long as we live, we will have hundreds of choices to make each day, and surely, there is a high probability of some missteps. Our objective is to take responsibility for all our choices, celebrate the wins, learn from our mistakes, correct what we can, and accept what we cannot, but no matter what, we keep moving forward.

"There is healing and power in saying, 'I made a choice, it was a mistake, I have no one to blame, it was my fault, I take responsibility, and now it's time to make a change.'"

Part IV: Seeking Comfort

Dear God,
I don't have to be okay all the time,
as long as I know You're here with me.
Comfort me with Your loving presence,
especially when it's cold and dark, and I feel alone.
Show me Your fingerprints in everything around me.

Chapter 12
Feel Free to Feel

It is possible to allow ourselves to feel various emotions and yet, not suffer. Negative emotions are unpleasant, but some people avoid experiencing even the positive ones for fear of the pain they might bring along. To feel loved and become successful, for example, can make a person happy and content. But because happiness does not last forever or long enough, these things can lead to loneliness and disappointment. To feel is human. The myriad of emotions that life brings enriches us and creates a profound human experience that transforms us. Those who refuse to feel because of the fear of suffering will realize that not feeling is suffering in itself. We are not machines that process information based on equations and data alone. Our humanity is connected to our ability to experience and show emotions. Our physical body can climb and run, but it is our soul that feels. Our body decays over time, but our soul continues to transform to a higher level of existence by being exposed to both positive and negative emotions. It is like a tree that grows deeper roots and stronger trunks after being subjected to the harsh elements. We should not be afraid of or resist emotions. They are a natural part of daily living and will ebb and flow, whether we like it or not. Our goal should not be to avoid them but instead, learn to manage them to our benefit rather than our detriment.

As dark colors contrast the bright in a painting, negative emotions enhance the value of positive ones. Furthermore, negative ones can serve as catalyst for change and growth. The grief from losing a loved one teaches us to value those we have around us. It reveals the depths to which we loved the person we lost. It reminds us of the brevity of life. It also tests our faith in God and our beliefs about God's promises. Anger can motivate us to change what is wrong around us and breed the passion to serve those who face the same. The pain and hurt caused by spouses and friends who betray us teach us how to evaluate people's characters and protect us from repeating the same mistake. Loneliness can lead us to search for and lean on God and experience His constant and reliable presence. Missing someone or longing for someone uncovers the love between two people that would otherwise be presupposed. Dealing with the stress of work, relationships, and struggles of daily life helps us develop resilience and strength to cope with future challenges. Anxiety about a health concern or financial difficulty can humble us; we learn that money cannot buy us health, and both are fleeting. The more important things in life become apparent, and our need for God becomes more urgent.

It is unhelpful to tell someone struggling with negative emotions not to dwell on those thoughts or try to convince them their concerns are invalid. And yet, many well-meaning people do this. Attempting to avoid thinking about a particular thing requires conscious thought, thereby making you think about it even more. Replacing a negative thought with a blissful one is worth a try, but it may not be sustainable. It takes a lot of effort to resist going back to the negative thoughts you are trying to replace. The struggling person's energy tank is already low; there may not be enough reserves to pull from. Although we have a choice whether to dwell on negative emotions and nurture them from a molehill to a mountain, we do not have control when they come or go; they are energies much like wind and light. How each person processes them depends on their past experiences and personality. Hence, it would be wrong and insensitive to tell someone they have no reason to feel the way they are feeling. It may give the person you are trying to comfort a false perception that you just do not want to help.

Waves in the ocean are created by the passage of wind energy through water. The turbulence created by the wind makes them rise, and as it dissipates, the waves fall. Emotions are the same external energies that pass through us and create turbulence, like the wind's effect on the water. They cause a burst of positive or negative energy and then fizzle out with time. They are passing forces that do not remain and are separate from us. Proof of this is we continue to exist even after the emotions pass. Therefore, we are not our emotions and should not identify as them. The physiologic changes we experience due to emotions are from the turbulence it creates in us. Once it passes, our body goes back to its steady state. It is essential to be aware that emotions are external energies that are merely passing through. Knowing that the turbulence it created is transient will help us cope better. Since emotions are energies, they cannot be seen; their effect on us is what we feel. The behavior we manifest because of the turbulence the energy created is what people see; this is the only part of this experience we can control. Understanding the anatomy of emotions, as I discussed above, can be comforting and reassuring. We realize that we are not our emotions. Therefore, experiencing them does not make us good or bad. It is how we choose to display the effect of the turbulence within that is judged by those who witness them. We know that emotions are energies that merely pass through us and are transitory. If we wait long enough, the energy will expend itself and subside. However, it is up to us how long we will nurture the effects of the turbulence and manifest them for the world to see.

To experience life at its fullest, we need to allow ourselves to feel the emotions that come our way. They enrich our life experiences and transform us into the person God intended. We must be careful not to let emotions destroy us or run our lives; instead, we need to learn how to manage them. They are necessary and natural, and we are better served to accept and interact productively with them rather than ignore them. Resisting what is natural causes us to suffer. Surfers do not fight the waves. They ride the various kinds of waves that come their way and interact with them lest they crash. Have the courage to feel. Take a chance at being happy and improve as a person, even if it requires temporary difficulty. Not all pain causes suffering if you choose to take the right perspective.

CHAPTER 13
WHEN YOU DON'T UNDERSTAND

We often want life to be status quo, stable, and predictable. Unfortunately, it is not. It is most devastating when life seems so good and suddenly, an unexpected tragedy happens. There are also times when things in life are exactly how we believe they should be, but later become something other than what we had hoped. These may be the untimely death or unforeseen illness of a loved one, the loss of your once sweet child to the consequences of wrong choices he made, or the breakup of a perfect relationship you thought was for a lifetime. The pain from these can be so overwhelming one may feel defeated. It is during these times that we scour for answers. We want to know why it happened, why it needed to happen, and why it happened to us. Unfortunately, those questions often go unanswered because there is not one. We then start seeking someone to blame. That often leaves us unsatisfied, so we turn inward and start blaming ourselves. When that attempt at finding peace fails, we turn our anger on God.

When you do not understand some things in life, be assured that it is not required. There are always things that cannot be explained. Some happen for no reason. Some questions have no answers. Some mysteries cannot be solved. We need to learn to accept that there are things we cannot understand at the moment and our hearts will be unsettled. Accepting does not mean we give up. It means we keep moving forward and continue living our lives, as we continue the search for answers. Being unsettled is a powerful driver in our search for meaning in our suffering. We may never find the answer that satisfies our logic, but if we find a purpose for our pain, our suffering will not be in vain. This is the beginning of faith, where we train our hearts to see when our eyes cannot.

It is human to be angry, sad, and confused when we hurt. Blaming God for the most complex and difficult issues in our lives is somehow an admission of our faith. We blame God because we acknowledge that He exists, He knows everything, with the power to do anything, and yet, He did not save us from the pain. It demonstrates that we believe God loves us but question why we are in this predicament if He truly does. This is a good place for us to start. We build our faith on what we believe is true; God exists, knows everything, can do anything, and loves us. In a moment of intense suffering, there is no need to overthink things. When you are overwhelmed, it is not the time to find the purpose for your suffering. Just hold on to what you know about God and patiently wait for Him to calm your heart. Psalm 34:18 says, *"The Lord is close to the brokenhearted and saves those who are crushed in spirit,"* and Psalm 147:13 says, *"He heals the brokenhearted and binds up their wounds."* God knows you are tired and weakened by the onslaught of unfortunate events. He does not require you to go looking for Him. He will find you where you are; all you need to do is welcome Him. From there, watch how the new chapter of your life unfolds and marvel at what God will do.

Suffering draws us closer to God. It reveals our inability to rely on ourselves; we are humbled and learn to depend on God. It shows us the importance of faith; we find hope when we decide to trust God. In 2 Corinthians 4:7-9, St. Paul said, *"But we have this treasure in jars of clay to show that this all-surpassing power is from God and not from us. We are hard pressed on every side, but not crushed; perplexed, but not in despair; persecuted, but not abandoned; struck down, but not destroyed."* Being in need allows us to experience the love and goodness of the people around us. This in turn, reveals God's loving presence. Suffering heightens our sensitivity to the needs of others. As a result, we live less for ourselves and more for them, and this is the beginning of a life of true happiness, peace, and contentment.

"He does not require you to go looking for Him. He will find you where you are; all you need to do is welcome Him."

CHAPTER 14
DEFENDING AGAINST OFFENSES

Each day, there are countless opportunities to be offended. We interact with many people, either in person or by electronic communications, and it is inevitable that some of the things they say or do, or things they do not say or do, would end up hurting our feelings. Those closest to us seem more likely to offend us, as it hurts most when it matters the most. For many, living in peace and harmony is the goal. Learning to be offense-proof is a major step to getting there.

We must realize and accept that we cannot control other people's actions. We can try to influence their behavior, but only they can determine the outcome. It is difficult enough to control ourselves and do what we know we should. Seeking to control others will surely end in disappointment and frustration. Determining whether we get offended is within our power and volition. Our focus should be on managing our responses and reactions, rather than controlling how others act. People around us decide whether to sling mud or throw garbage at us. We choose whether to let the mud stick or take the garbage home. *"A person's wisdom yields patience; it is to one's glory to overlook an offense* (Proverbs 19:11)."

Go Higher. Others will try to offend, and we should try not to be offended. If we were a target, we could go higher to avoid getting hit. It is easier to shoot a target at close range and eye level rather than one that is further out and higher. Just because other people descend to a dark place does not mean we must do the same. We can choose to fight fire with fire and claim we are only human or decide to live an enlightened life, experience more joy, and lessen our pain. *"If you are sensible, you will control your temper. When someone wrongs you, it is a great virtue to ignore it* (Proverbs 19:11)." Even if it is difficult to continue doing what is right and good, and to love and forgive in the face of mistreatment, the alternative is not better. Seeking revenge is draining. Plotting revenge alone consumes our energy, and dealing with its consequences heightens our unhappiness. We do what is right and good because it is in our nature to do so. We love and forgive because we want peace from choosing this path, not because the offender is deserving. Loving our enemies means we are willing to give them the benefit of our doubt and believe they did the wrong things because they didn't know any better at the time. We accept them for who they are at that moment and make no judgments. Hopefully, as they know better, they will behave better. In the meantime, we should also allow ourselves to experience the normal human emotions of anger and hurt but be careful not to let them lead us to sin. *"In your anger do not sin. Do not let the sun go down while you are still angry, and do not give the devil a foothold* (Ephesians 4:26-27)." Our firm but reasonable and controlled response to their misdeeds can hopefully discourage and teach the offender not to repeat them. Despite the challenge, we should try to pray for their well-being and enlightenment, and for ourselves, pray for strength and kindness to show grace. Forgiving them does not mean we pretend the offense never happened. It just means giving others another chance and not writing them off. *"Everyone should be quick to listen, slow to speak and slow to become angry, because human anger does not produce the righteousness that God desires* (James 1:19-20)." It is challenging to change bad habits and behaviors we've repeated for a long time; we are likely to offend again and again because of them. Understanding our own frailty helps us make allowances for the failings of others and lessen our concern about others' recurring offenses. We forgive when the opportunity presents itself, just as we hope others will forgive us when we need it. When the same offenses are committed, our job is to try to forgive again, and their job is to try not to do it again. Give people time to grow, and trust that they will either get better or naturally drift away from you on their own. If they get better, you earn a friend. If they drift away, you rid yourself of a recurring heartache without the added pain of forcing it to happen.

Keep moving. A moving target is harder to hit. People can say or do things to us that should hurt, but if our minds are pre-occupied with better things and we are not even aware that we are supposed to hurt, there would not be any damage done. Avoid idle time; time spent licking our wounds is idle time. It is unproductive and wastes precious time. This would leave us stuck in a dark place, stunt our growth, and make us easy targets for more hurts. It is important to stay busy living life and pay attention to things that matter; we should keep moving forward. Life is short and there are a lot of people in this world who need and appreciate us. We would be remiss if we neglected them because we are too busy feeling sorry for ourselves and trying to get even with people who try to hurt us. Spend your time wisely and direct your energy to people who value you and whose lives you could enhance.

Stay slick. WD-40 is a popular multi-purpose spray in America that displaces moisture and lubricates almost anything. This product is commonly used to spray off-road vehicles to prevent mud and clay from clinging and hardening on the surface. We, too, must always keep ourselves lubricated to avoid holding on to the mud people throw at us. It took the creators forty attempts to perfect the formulation of this product, hence the name WD-40 (Water Displacement perfected on the 40th try). We must prepare ourselves to handle offenses before the opportunity presents itself. Soldiers do not learn to shoot only when face-to-face with the enemy, nor do athletes train the night before a competition. Preparation is key. We do not wait until we have been offended before we figure out how to deal with it. Incidents that can potentially be offensive will happen to everyone; expect it. How we respond depends on how prepared we are. We need to have a strategy for dealing with specific situations. We should seek wisdom and enlightenment regularly through prayer and meditation, reading the scriptures and other books from authors we admire and trust, listening to teachings on various topics that pique our curiosity, and learning from people with great insights are good ways to learn. To be better at anything, we need practice. We should practice forgiving, practice gratitude, practice serving others, and practice thinking of ourselves less. Finally, we need to learn to welcome the sufferings we face in life as an opportunity to learn patience, resilience, and how to truly love.

Wash it off. It is important to wash off the mud as soon as we realize we have it on us. Leaving it for an extended period will cause it to dry up and harden, making it difficult to remove. When people offend us, we should allow ourselves to feel anger; that is normal and should not be suppressed. However, we need to be mindful of how we act when angry. Sometimes, it is better not to act at all. We should treat the emotion of anger as a visitor coming through our doors. Wait for it to leave before we decide what to say or do. We often say the wrong things and act inappropriately when angry, and almost certainly, end up with regrets. It is important to recognize that feeling offended is not the problem. Offending someone is. The person who offended you, whether intentionally or not, is the one who has an issue that needs resolution. You are not weak because you felt offended; it is the offender who could not control himself who is. We do not need to seek forgiveness when we are offended, for there is nothing to forgive. Letting go of an offense as quickly as possible is the best thing we could do to help us heal. We should not hold on to the offense even if it makes us feel self-righteous. Being angry over someone else's mistake does not make us better people. Why hold on to the garbage other people throw at us? Why bring it home with us? That garbage bag is heavy and smells; over time, it will embitter and wear us out. The people around us who love, need, and value us would not want to be around us nor would they benefit from us when we are in this condition. Wash off the mud, and do not pick up the garbage people throw at us. We should not dwell on the offense or allow it to stick. If we cannot remove the offender from our lives, we can at least limit our exposure to them, lower our expectations, or expect nothing from them. After we deal with our hurts and the anger resulting from it, we need to promptly move on and make room to focus on what really matters and find the many reasons out there that make us feel free and truly happy.

"Determining whether we get offended is within our power and volition. Our focus should be on managing our responses and reactions, rather than controlling how others act."

PART V: SEEKING CONSOLATION

Dear God,
As I face challenges and disappointments,
it is difficult to see beyond the hurt.
Help me see things from your viewpoint
and find purpose in my pain.
Bestow on me Your wisdom
that I may know my growth depends on them.

CHAPTER 15
YOU DON'T OWE ME ANYTHING

Have you ever felt unappreciated? Have you ever given everything to help someone only to be forgotten when your help was no longer needed? Have you ever loved someone without holding back only to find yourself alone when the extraordinary love you gave became ordinary? The pain from this can be deep, and it can discourage you from helping and loving others to avoid suffering again. Being kind to others can never be a mistake. The error lies in the person who mishandled your generous act of love. You should not stop loving, giving, and being kind, just because of this. This did not happen because you were not judicious in selecting who to help; it happened because people change. Some act differently when they are in need. Sickness, unemployment, loneliness, failure, and helplessness make people thoughtful, sensitive, seemingly sincere, and appreciative because they are vulnerable and need you. Genuine people are those who remain the same way even after their situation improves. It is right to help someone who is in need. We are always to love fully those God put in our lives. We cannot only choose to love the ones we think are genuine because we would not know who they are until their true intentions manifest after their crisis has passed. It is better to love, help, and be kind to someone and look like a fool than miss out on helping someone who truly needs and deserves it just because we want to avoid getting hurt. In Proverbs 3:27-28, it says, *"Do not withhold good from those to whom it is due, when it is in your power to act. Do not say to your neighbor, "Come back tomorrow and I'll give it to you" – when you already have it with you."* No one would knowingly allow someone to take advantage of them. We all use our best judgment based on the facts available to us at the time. Sometimes, there is just no way to know. This should not stop us from living life fully and loving others generously. If we know the why's of what we do, we would be willing to take risks to love and be good to others whenever necessary.

We find meaning in life when we serve others. Nelson Henderson once said, *"The true meaning of life is to plant trees, under whose shade you do not expect to sit."* Unless we live for something outside of seeking our own happiness, nothing we do will satisfy us. There is something to be said about being kind and helpful to others; it makes us feel alive, happy, and content. Genuine service is not transactional; we do not help or give hoping to receive something in return. Loving others can yield profound and lasting satisfaction, especially if we give it freely to someone undeserving and do not expect a positive reception. We are human, and it is natural to seek appreciation from others. Although it is disappointing when people we helped take us for granted, we often eventually get over it. Once we have experienced the joy of loving unconditionally and selflessly, our disappointment will turn into empathy and concern for the other, and our pain will lead to personal growth and maturity. I help others because it makes me happy. So, to those I have helped in my lifetime, you don't owe me anything.

In 1 Peter 4:8, it says, *"Above all, love each other deeply, because love covers over a multitude of sins."* I am a sinner, and I have sinned seven times seventy-seven times, and more; that is a lot of sins to cover. Hence, I take every opportunity to love and be kind to make up for my shortcomings, not as a punishment but a chance to show repentance and indirectly make amends. In a way, this is like investing in a spiritual savings account from which I can draw graces from when I need them. So, to those I have loved in my lifetime, you don't owe me anything.

To deeply care for someone and not be reciprocated can be very discouraging. The wounds from this can be deep, but they will eventually heal and be replaced with scars. Scars bury the wounds, and their strength keeps them from reopening. Making sacrifices for others out of love is risky; we give up a part of ourselves for the benefit of others. The more we give, the more it will hurt when what we give is not appreciated or is quickly forgotten. There is benefit in having experienced this pain. It teaches us to show gratitude for the love we receive from others. It builds our character and helps us learn to be okay regardless of what others decide to do or not do. It leads us to seek the lasting satisfaction of God's approval instead of human applause. In the process, it deepens our faith. Caring for others benefits me as much as it fills the needs of others. So, to those I have cared for in my lifetime, you don't owe me anything.

People have been kind to me, loved me, helped me, and cared for me. They enriched my life in more ways than one and their actions allowed me to experience God's love. Despite this, I am sure I have disappointed some in my lifetime. God loves me unconditionally, and I have failed Him more times than I can count. Despite that, He has blessed me generously beyond what I deserve. It is my turn to pay forward the kindness, love, help, and care I received from others. It is my turn to give back to God by serving the people He sends my way. I am very thankful for each opportunity to serve others and lead them to God. The sacrifices required of me in doing this are hopefully at least commensurate to the love I received from others and an acceptable thanksgiving offering to God. So, to those whom I have served and somehow led to God in my lifetime, you don't owe me anything.

If we only do good to others when we know we will be rewarded, that is not service and is lacking love. If we engage in transactional acts of love, prepare to be disappointed. It is natural to seek recognition and expect reciprocation for what we give, but the lack of guarantee should not keep us from doing so. To hedge against disappointment and hurt, we need to remind ourselves constantly that people do not owe us anything. Even if people ask us for help, we always have the option to say "no." We chose to help because we benefit from doing so. An inherent reward is attached to doing good; the joy derived from the act itself is already compensation. Additional payment from the recipient of our goodwill is not required, and we are not entitled to it. So, the next time someone whom you have loved deeply and helped generously turns their back on you after they got what they needed, give them a pass, and say, "you don't owe me anything."

CHAPTER 16
EXPECTATIONS

L ife is fluid and full of surprises. It constantly changes, and things happen without our permission. We can insist on how things should be, but life does not necessarily follow our wishes or expectations. We can do everything within our power to direct life according to our limited wisdom, but we will not always succeed. Every person around us is unique. No two people are entirely alike. There may be similarities between them, but they are never a perfect match. We often expect others to think and behave like us, but it always disappoints. We can never control how others act or change them to fit our mold. Furthermore, people also change, and we may not like what they become. Their core self may not be as fluid, but everything else is malleable. People adapt to their environment, and their experiences transform them. It is often said that we should avoid having expectations in life and people, lest we end up disillusioned. But it is human to expect something in return for what we invest. It is healthy to have expectations because it is a byproduct of having hope in something. Hope is the very essence that motivates us to live life to the fullest. Avoiding expectations is not the objective, but rather, learning to manage them to where we can accept an outcome even if it is contrary to what we desire. This helps us maintain the balance we need to live a satisfying life.

I know of teachers who dedicate their entire lives to educating children. They do this because they love what they do and find satisfaction in molding the future of other people's children. I am sure some of them have been disappointed when kids they mentored never returned to say, *"thank you,"* after they graduated and became successful in their careers.

I know of people who saw their jobs as a ministry and vocation. They went to work early, worked overtime to get tasks done, gave everything they had, remained loyal to their bosses, and never bothered to ask for a raise. Yet, their effort and dedication remained unnoticed, but their little mistakes were highlighted promptly. I know of business owners who gave up opportunities to make a profit to be good stewards of their money and help give their employees a chance to have a better life. I am sure it must have been disappointing when their employees left when they were needed most because a better opportunity was presented to them elsewhere. I have invested in friendships where the line between us was blurred, and I nurtured them as if they were part of me. Unfortunately, over time, what was once extraordinary became ordinary, life became busy, and the value of our relationship became less than the pull of new adventures. Some people ate well, exercised regularly, lived a healthy lifestyle, and got regular check-ups from their doctors. Yet, they somehow fell ill unexpectedly. I know of people who dedicated their lives to serving God, did extraordinary things, and gave up their own comfort and needs for the sake of others. Still, they have unfortunate things happen to them. We go to school, study hard, and expect a high-paying job after graduation. Sadly, the hard work did not pay off for some, and they ended up doing something other than what they invested time, money, and effort to become. Many people are programmed to believe that the normal progression of life should be to go to school, get a job, get married, and have children. However, the reality is, some people never get to marry, and some are not blessed with children. Life is unpredictable. Many things are beyond our control. What we get may not always be commensurate with what we give. People and circumstances constantly change. Those we hold dear come and go. The difference between "what was" and "what is" can be a minute. We must be aware of this truth to avoid being caught off guard when it happens.

It is natural for us to expect appreciation from people we have helped. Most, if not all, help others because it is the right thing to do, and it is in their nature to help. I am certain they also derive pleasure and happiness doing it, but that does not take away the nobleness of their action. The expectation of being appreciated was created by one's experiences. Those who had been helped expressed their gratitude to the giver out of the fullness of their hearts, and thought it was a natural response. Those who received appreciation from people they helped realized how great it felt to be recognized and want to experience the same again; reward breeds desire for repetition and creates expectations. Our minds are then programmed to appreciate and be appreciated. Hence, it became part of societal norms and tenets of basic human decency. The problem herein lies with the ungrateful person who acted outside the norms, not the Good Samaritan who expected appreciation. His disappointment is a natural emotion, not a manifestation of selfishness, manipulation, or insincerity. However, it is essential to learn how to manage these letdowns to prevent hurt and discouragement.

Many of us were taught from childhood to set goals and work diligently toward achieving them. Many seek their purpose in life and channel their time, energy, and talents to fulfill it. We find driven and motivated people very inspiring, and we want to emulate them. The *"If I can dream it, I can achieve it"* mentality often sets us up to expect lofty results from our hard work. There is also this transactional mindset where we believe that good things should happen to people who do good. Many of us also tend to think that the prevailing opinion of what is good is true. All these contribute to forming many of our expectations in life. This kind of thinking, however, does not consider that God is in control of everything, and our desires will be fulfilled only if it aligns with God's will. It also does not consider that there is redemptive value in withholding blessings or allowing failures in our lives, in much the same way we discipline our children because we love them.

Dealing effectively with unmet expectations rests solely on how we think and react. We cannot depend on other people or circumstances to satisfy us. Life happens to us and not for us. We cannot dictate what life ought to be nor demand how others should treat us. Our willingness to accept whatever life brings gives us the fortitude to face the possibility of disappointment in having expectations.

We should accept everything that happens as if that is the way it is supposed to be, because it is. There is no alternative. We cannot alter what has already happened. It is futile to reject reality. We do not have control of things outside of ourselves. The only things we can control are our thoughts and reactions. Therefore, we should do what we intend in life, embrace our expectations, and prepare to accept whatever outcome. We should let our expectations motivate us to pursue our intentions with passion. Should the outcome be other than what we desired, we should be humble enough to accept that not everything will go our way, be proud that we dared to pursue our purpose, and be grateful for the experience. It is natural to be disappointed, but staying disappointed is not beneficial or healthy. What is happening in the present moment is the only reality. Accepting this allows us to see things for what they are and determine what options are available to us. Acceptance is not acquiescence or surrender. It is engaging and interacting with what is happening, like a surfer riding a wave. Resisting life or rejecting reality is akin to a surfer trying to stop the wave, fighting it, and crashing. If we determine that there is something we can do to change or improve, that is where we should direct our time and energy. If we cannot alter our circumstances, we should not dwell on it in self-pity and should move on to more productive endeavors. If there is no satisfactory answer to our dilemma, it is not wrong to sit still and wait for clarity. Waiting is still an act of doing. Patience will serve us better than reckless and indiscriminate actions that might end up causing unintended damage.

It is important to accept that other people are different from us and accept them for who they are. We cannot expect them to think like us, act like us, and respond to things like us. Furthermore, we cannot control them and make them become like us; this will only lead to frustration. Even if we agree with others now, be cognizant that people change. It is okay to have expectations of others, but we should be open to accepting disappointments. Most of our expectations are usually met because we tend to gravitate toward people who think like us. People who are significantly different tend to naturally drift apart. But the rare disagreements between like-minded individuals cause the most heartaches. These are the instances where we have an opportunity to grow. We must learn to focus on what we can do, not what we think others should do. We must modify how we think and react toward others when they fail to meet our expectations, rather than force them to do what we expect.

We do not need to create arbitrary expectations by defining what is good and what makes us happy. We should accept whatever is given to us, be thankful for them, and expect to be pleased with whatever we receive. If we do not define happiness based on our marital status or number of children, we can be content whether we are single or married, and whether we have children or not. If we do not define what makes life good, we can be satisfied even if we are alone, sick, or poor. We should have the faith and humility to believe that life itself, and everything that comes with it, are gifts from God. We deserve nothing, are entitled to nothing, and all we receive is icing on the cake. Knowing that they are blessings and graces freely bestowed on us, we become grateful and happier.

Having expectations in life is essential. It gives us something to hope for. It can motivate us to overcome difficulties. It is not something we should avoid to spare ourselves hurt and disappointment. It does not indicate insincerity and does not lessen the merit and purity of our intentions. When allowing ourselves to have expectations, it is vital to be prepared that some of them will not be met. The openness to accept that everything is happening the way it is supposed to be will guard our hearts against disappointment and discouragement. We should accept others for who they are or what they become, and receive everything that comes our way, good or bad, as a gift we need to be thankful for.

CHAPTER 17
IT'S ALL TAKEN CARE OF

You have been caring for a loved one who has been sick for a while now. You must be physically exhausted, staying up late at night watching her and ensuring she is okay. Mentally, you are drained just trying to be understanding and not letting her sarcasm frustrate you. It also requires a lot of effort to act bravely to cover your anxiety and avoid worrying others; this is debilitating you. You cannot see the light at the end of the tunnel, and you do not even know if there is one. As you sat down and prayed, Jesus whispered, *"If you remain in me and my words remain in you, you may ask for anything you want, and it will be granted* (John 15:7)." So, you took a deep breath and consciously felt life fill your being as you inhaled. Without assigning words to how you felt, you experienced a deep sense of gratitude for the gift of life that allowed you to breathe. As you exhaled, you felt your anxiety and the weight of the world leave your body through your nostrils. You then decided to keep trusting God, even if the future of your loved one remained uncertain. You continue to ask God for help. You continue to seek God's comforting presence. You keep knocking on the door to God's heart. The Holy Spirit brought forth to your mind Jesus' words when He said, *"Come to me, all of you who are weary and carry heavy burdens, and I will give you rest* (Matthew 11:28)." You kept those words in your heart and accepted His invitation.

Through all the pain you endured as you watched your loved one struggle with her illness, you remained in God and His words remained in you. You are confident that God will keep His promise to grant you whatever you request. But what do you really want to ask of God? I am sure you want your loved one healed so that you can enjoy the good old days with her again, don't you? As you work through the doubts and uncertainties in your mind, you are reassured of God's generosity and love for you. He gave you the gift of life; you became fully aware of this when you consciously took a breath. We often take this for granted when we are feeling well. Unlike your loved one, you could take that breath without difficulty. You were grateful to be blessed like this, despite recalling the times you were less than lovable when you strayed from the path God desired for you. Because God first loved you, you trusted Him. You came to know His character through His words from the scriptures. You learned that He is all-knowing and all-powerful. You realize that He is faithful and keeps His promises. So, you decided to let God be God, and let His perfect will be done, not yours. Consequently, what became more important to you was for your loved one to be at peace, to feel the loving presence of God, and not feel alone. It does not really matter to you how God will accomplish them as long as He does. You also shifted your petitions to asking God for strength and courage as you answered His call to minister to your loved one. You asked God to bless you with quality time with her and make memories you can cherish for the rest of your life. You asked God to give you enough faith to keep trusting Him. As you asked for all these specific things, it became clear what you really wanted from God. You ceased to demand that He heals your loved one, although that was still your hope for her. Calmness and peace replaced the anxiety and panic that paralyzed you, as you entrusted the future of your loved one to God.

As you finished your prayer and meditation, you opened your eyes and looked at your loved one. She was still sick, but she seemed at peace. She was still weak, but she looked comfortable. She was lying in bed, but you were right beside her. You were exhausted, but you could attend to her needs. You were anxious, but you still had the presence of mind to watch over her. You could not go to work, but you were grateful you had the opportunity to spend time alone with her. Your family and friends know what you are going through. They are in awe at how you are able to keep everything together. Based on all that, it is glaringly apparent that God must have granted all you had petitioned.

"Calmness and peace replaced the anxiety and panic that paralyzed you, as you entrusted the future of your loved one to God."

Part VI: Seeking a Better World

Dear God,
I want to help others experience Your love
and see the beauty of life.
Teach me to be kind and generous
that they may understand Your love through mine.
Give me the passion to make this the purpose of my life.

CHAPTER 18
ALL WE NEED IS LOVE

John Lennon from the English rock band, "The Beatles", wrote the song, "All You Need is Love." The single was released in July of 1967 and became a number-one hit on the Billboard Chart at the time. In the song, he wrote, *"Nothing you can make that can't be made. No one you can save that can't be saved. All you need is love. Love is all you need."* This theme resonated 55 years ago. Today, it is as relevant as it was then. There are a lot of people hurting around us. Many never say a word. Some people feign happiness to hide the pain inside. Some exude negativity as a means to cope. Some people simply have no one to turn to for support, and their remaining option is to surrender. If we want to make this world a better place, maybe more love is what we need. If we want to make a difference in a person's life, maybe love is what we need to give. Love is the one investment in life that multiplies only when you give it away. This is truly one of life's greatest ironies. If we want our emotional bank to be full, the most cost-efficient thing to do is to love more; we need to love more deeply and freely. There are endless opportunities around us. We just need to be more attuned to their existence. If we do not look for them, we may not find them. The act does not have to be big. We do not need to travel to far flung places to find someone to love. We do not need to raise a million dollars to donate to make a difference. It is the co-worker whose elderly mom is sick, and she is worried about losing her and her job. It is the opponent across the tennis court from you who was rude because he is tired of losing on the court and in life. It is the waitress at the restaurant who gave you less than five-star service because her mind was preoccupied with raising her child as a single mom. It is the friend who remains single and pushes you away because he does not want to be reminded of being alone while watching you lead a "normal" life with your wife and kids. It is the person who feels ostracized by society because they do not look like you, eat the same food as you, love like you, or sound like you when they speak. It is the person whose son is a drug addict who withdraws from you because she is ashamed, and at the same time, worried that her son might overdose. It is the neighbor who cannot bring their trash bin back in because their child has been sick in the hospital for months. It is the young widow who feels less worthy because she is alone and does not attend school functions with a man beside her. It is the person suffering from an unknown illness none of her doctors can figure out who never feels well. It could be your puppy who waits for you all day to come home and rub her belly. You must have encountered one of these at some point in your life. It is easy to love those who love us back or loved us first. It is easy to love those who are lovable. But the people who are not easy to love are the ones who need it most. Jesus said in Luke 6:32, *"If you love only those who love you, why should you get credit for that? Even sinners love those who love them!"* He continued in Luke 6:35-36 saying, *"Love your enemies! Do good to them. Lend to them without expecting to be repaid. Then your reward from heaven will be very great, and you will truly be acting as children of the Most High, for He is kind to those who are unthankful and wicked. You must be compassionate, just as your Father is compassionate."* Let us challenge ourselves to consciously look for someone to love each day by showing kindness without needing a reason.

"*Love is the one investment in life that multiplies only when you give it away.*"

CHAPTER 19
LUCEAT LUX -- SHINE THE LIGHT

Jesus said, *"I am the light of the world. Whoever follows me will not walk in darkness but will have the light of life* (John 8:12)."

Rick Warren, author of "The Purpose Driven Life" and founder of Saddleback Church, made one of the most remarkable statements when his youngest son, Matthew, took his own life after struggling with depression for many years. When asked in an interview how he was dealing with this tragedy, he said, *"I do not need an explanation from God. I just need God."* Many people around us struggle with loneliness, hopelessness, and pain of all kinds. They long for the dark nights to end, the sun to rise, and hope to get some relief from their suffering. Even a brief respite is welcome; a chance to breathe and find strength to last another day. All the clichés that well-meaning people like to say, such as "God is good," "God is in control," or "God loves you," sometimes seem disingenuous; they can make the situation worse. Whenever I pray for someone who is suffering, my prayer is simply that the person feels the presence of God. God has His will, and I trust in His perfect plan. My only desire is for the person to have the strength to emerge from the storm unscathed. One's sense of suffering from whatever cause is a vague and subjective emotional affliction, and each person deals with it differently. Comforting someone cannot be effectively done using logic or by pointing out the lack of reason for their pain. The only way to dispel the perception of darkness in the suffering person's mind is to replace it with an overwhelming experience of love. When our acts of kindness show the person in need that we genuinely care, we help them feel the presence of God. In this state of divine awareness, the person can transcend the pain and acknowledge the suffering without experiencing its sting. People will not believe that God is good and cares for them just because we say so. They will only believe that God truly loves them and will sustain them because of the love we make them feel. When we imitate how Jesus treated people, we shine His light on others and allow them to understand the kind of love He gives. In turn, they feel God's love flow to them through us. Indeed, Jesus is the light of the world who can dispel the darkness in our lives.

To be more like Jesus, we need to know how He lived His life and learn about His teachings. In the gospel of John 4:7-10, Jesus reached out to a Samaritan woman despite the prevailing tradition at the time which barred Jews from interacting with other races. In Luke 19:1-9, not only did Jesus reach out to Zacchaeus, an outcast of society because of his dishonesty as a tax-collector, He even invited Himself to be Zacchaeus's guest in his home. In John 8:3-11, when the teachers of the law brought in a woman caught in adultery for Jesus to condemn, He surprised them by saying, *"Let any one of you who is without sin be the first to throw a stone at her."* After all her accusers left, Jesus asked her, *"Woman, where are they? Has no one condemned you? Then neither do I condemn you. Go now and leave your life of sin."* In John 11:1-37, Jesus comforted Mary and Martha when their brother Lazarus died. Jesus *"was deeply moved in spirit and troubled,"* and wept. In Luke 23:32-43, at His crucifixion, Jesus prayed for the people who tortured and murdered Him saying, *"Father, forgive them, for they know not what they do."* And to one of the criminals crucified beside him who said, *"Jesus, remember me when you come into your Kingdom,"* he replied, *"I assure you, today you will be with me in paradise."* Jesus showed us by His examples how we can shine His light on others and be the light illuminating the path that leads to Him. Every day, we are presented with many opportunities to accept His invitation to be the light for others.

In Romans 12:6-8 St. Paul said, *"God has given us different gifts for doing certain things well. So, if God has given you the ability to prophesy, speak out with as much faith as God has given you. If your gift is serving others, serve them well. If you are a teacher, teach well. If your gift is to encourage others, be encouraging. If it is giving, give generously. If God has given you leadership ability, take the responsibility seriously. And if you have a gift for showing kindness to others, do it gladly."* Many people I have come to know have inspired me with their selfless acts of service. They serve God by serving others. They shine God's light on the world through their acts of kindness and love. We all serve God in diverse ways, and every form of service is equal in importance in the eyes of God. My friend and co-worker cut down her work hours significantly to become the sole caretaker of her two elderly parents who have serious chronic medical problems. They were in and out of the hospital and back and forth to the doctor's clinic. Their daily needs consumed her days and nights. My cousin's wife takes care of her father-in-law as if he is her own father. He is elderly and has serious medical problems, and her dedication is unparalleled. She has her own medical issues too, but it seems like she puts his needs above hers. One of my business partners has four children of his own, and he and his wife adopted three more to help give them a better future. They sacrificed their own comfort to enhance the lives of three less fortunate children. My wife is ever the giver. She gives generously to those who are in need, whether they are family or strangers. She has a tender heart by God's design. One of my closest friends has a wife and three young children and runs a small business. Even when he is tired from work or doing housework, he plays with the kids when they ask him, and he never skips bathing them or putting them to bed every night. His kids need him, and he is always there for them. God entrusted him with those children, and he serves God by caring for them like God wants him to. I know a nun who is also a friend. Her life in the convent is simple and devoid of most of the modern conveniences we enjoy. She dedicated her life to educating less fortunate children. She goes wherever the Mother Superior assigns her to serve. Hers is a life of self-denial. Truly, a life lived for others. All these people answered God's call to serve Him. They all chose to be the light for someone's world.

In Matthew 5:14-16 Jesus said, *"You are the light of the world. A town built on a hill cannot be hidden. Neither do people light a lamp and put it under a bowl. Instead, they put it on its stand, and it gives light to everyone in the house. In the same way, let your light shine before others, that they may see your good deeds and glorify your Father in heaven."* Let us be the ones who would love those the world rejects, those who are not easy to love, and those who do not love us back. Let us be the ones who would do what is right, even if the world says it is impractical, costly, and risky. Let us be the ones who would speak for those who do not have a voice, defend those who do not have strength, and meet the needs of those who do not have the means to do it on their own. Let us be the light of the world and make a difference in the lives of others, one person at a time.

Part VII: Seeking a Better Me

Dear God,
In order for me to serve You well,
I need to become a better person myself.
Reveal to me my faults and deficiencies
so that I may correct them.
Give me humility, strength, and determination
to act upon Your revelation.

Chapter 20
Be Gentle

Modern-day living is highly competitive, such that being gentle is not encouraged; it is perceived as weakness. Instead, people are taught at an early age to be assertive, bullish, demanding, and unyielding. In Matthew 5:5, Jesus said, *"Blessed are the meek, for they will inherit the earth."* To be gentle or meek is to know that we have the strength to do something but have the self-mastery to decide not to act because it is unnecessary. It shows the strength of one's character and resolve, instead of weakness.

When we disagree with the opinion of others, our natural tendency is to let them know we are right, and they are wrong. When others offend us, our instinct is to retaliate and repay them for the wrong they have done. The societal norm is to be firm, forceful, have clear intent, and strong resolve. Although this may be necessary for certain situations, a gentle approach is sometimes more desirable, possibly more effective, and may be all that is needed. A trained soldier with combat skills to win battles does not need to utilize those skills when dealing with a misbehaving toddler. In the appropriate situation, being gentle or meek is not a weakness. We do not always need to yell to be heard. We do not always need to demand to get results. We do not always need to coerce others to persuade. Sometimes, less is more. As a gastroenterologist who performs colonoscopies, I have learned that reaching the top of the colon requires more than just constantly pushing the scope. Often, it requires pulling the scope back first to propel it forward. It feels good for the massage therapist to pound our muscles into submission. However, I have learned it is more effective to apply intense pressure followed by briefly letting up to allow blood flow to the muscles, thereby clearing toxins that cause muscles to spasm. Similarly, cooking beef stew cannot be rushed with high fire. Proverbs 15:1 says, *"A gentle answer turns away wrath, but a harsh word stirs up anger."* Hard as it may be, resisting the desire to be blunt and opting instead to be gentle can spare us from unnecessary headaches and frustrations, and may even help us attain our objectives. It can calm an angry person and put to shame a cold-hearted offender.

Even when we know someone is wrong, we do not need to correct people constantly. And when others do not agree with our beliefs, we do not need to continue arguing our point until they acquiesce. It is responsible for us to share the truth as we know it, but it is not necessary to make everyone agree. We do not always need to have the last word. It is okay to let people believe they "won" an argument, even if we know they did not. When someone desperately wants something that rightly belongs to us, and sacrificing it is relatively inconsequential, give it up. When pursuing a goal could cause suffering for the people we love or care about and abdicating only means losing an opportunity or a mere inconvenience, let it go. Being gentle does not mean we do not pursue, persevere, or fight. It is choosing not to, even if we can, because it is not worthwhile. It takes strength of character to abandon a low-hanging fruit in deference to a belief in a higher purpose such as loving others. Love is an abstract concept made tangible by acts of gentleness, kindness, mercy, and patience. By practicing them, we learn how to love and live a deeply satisfying life.

While focusing on being gentle towards others is essential, learning to be gentle to ourselves is paramount. Often, we are our harshest critics. We constantly reprimand ourselves for every little mistake and deny ourselves the grace we typically show others. If we accept ourselves for who we are, we wouldn't need to seek approval from others. Until we learn to be truly gentle to ourselves, we will never be able to do the same for others. We live with ourselves twenty-four hours a day, seven days a week, and there is no escaping. To be happy, we should be to ourselves the best kind of friend we would like to have.

Be gentle to everyone, including ourselves. This way, life will be peaceful at home, at work, and in the community. We will be happier and more productive. This counter-culture proposition will not be easy to achieve as it has been disavowed by those around us. The only motivation that will sustain our efforts to be consistently gentle to the people around us is the desire to please God. To be gentle is to be loving, just as God wants us to be.

"*Being gentle does not mean we do not pursue, persevere, or fight. It is choosing not to, even if we can, because it is not worthwhile.*"

CHAPTER 21
WHY JUDGE?

We are all unique individuals who come from diverse backgrounds, have diverse life experiences, and possess individual strengths and weaknesses. We are all created equally imperfect. There is no reasonable way to decide which flaws are worse than others. Yet, we judge each other based on an arbitrary standard derived from our acquired random personal preferences and our subjective belief of how things should be. These standards we use to judge others may be faulty by nature. Because I randomly decided I liked the color blue, I could potentially judge those who prefer other colors as having poor taste. I work long hours and stay up late at night to pursue my dreams. This does not mean I am more diligent than those who approach life differently, but I could potentially judge them as lazy or unmotivated. However, others may think it is a bad idea that I burn the candle on both ends and subject my body to extreme stress. The only standard that matters in judging right or wrong, good or bad, acceptable or unacceptable, desirable or undesirable, is God's. The human mind is limited and biased, hence, incapable of making this determination.

Matthew 19:30: "But many who are first will be last, and many who are last will be first." Being judgmental is the result of an unchecked ego. We judge others when we entertain ourselves with the delusion of being morally and intellectually superior. We believe we can do no wrong and have done no wrong. We cannot imagine how we can make mistakes when we work diligently to pursue knowledge, and be disciplined, meticulous, and attentive to our tasks. Condemning others gives us the false assurance that we are better than them. It also shifts our guilt to someone else and fools us into believing that we are righteous.

We really do not have any right to judge anyone unless we know every facet of their life and have all the facts available to formulate the correct conclusion. It is unfair to look at one small truth and make a generalization about a person. Even if we try, it is not possible to really know what is truly going on in the lives of those we meet. Some people walk around with smiles on their faces, and yet, they may be suffering tremendously. Some people can be crude or distant on the surface, but they may have the kindest hearts. We just never know. No one would be willing to fully divulge to acquaintances or even non-close friends about all that is happening in their lives. Why would they or should they? They do not owe us an explanation for anything. Even the best of friends or spouses are sometimes unwilling to make themselves completely vulnerable and share with the other all their deepest thoughts, insecurities, pain, and other emotions. Some things we want to keep to ourselves. We all reserve a space in our hearts and minds that only God and we can tap.

Judging serves no purpose; it changes or fixes nothing. It only allows you to state you are right and the other person is wrong, regardless of its merit. If our goal is to help someone see the truth, hoping they make changes in their ways, we should approach them with love and kindness. Being judgmental makes people defensive and unwilling to listen. Pointing out the truth to others should be an objective discussion of only the facts. There is no need to add adjectives when stating the truth. There is no need to give an opinion, advice, or criticism unless asked. There is no need to formulate a conclusion or judgment about the truth being discussed. Even if we think we are one hundred percent right about an issue, we do not need to force our opinion on others. We need to remember that correcting someone is an act of love while judging others is a self-aggrandizing action. An act of love is selfless; hence, the goal is the good of others. We should live and let live. What other people ultimately decide about their lives is their choice. Our God-dictated responsibilities are to offer help, make ourselves available, and live our lives in such a way as to inspire people and draw them to a life of righteousness. Each moment we spend judging others is a moment lost to work on our shortcomings and improve ourselves. Each time we judge others with our own arbitrary standard of how to live, we set ourselves up to be discouraged when we fail to meet those measurement ourselves.

Imagine yourself sitting in front of five people you only know superficially. You were called in by this committee to be judged, without your solicitation. You do not work for them or owe them anything and are under no obligation to be under their scrutiny. Each of them will have five minutes to say what they think about any aspect of you. Either side will ask no questions, and you will not be allowed to make any statements. You will simply listen to what they have to say. Do you think any of them might say something untrue about you? Do you think any of them might judge you harshly or unfairly about something? Would you be happier if you did not have to sit in front of five mere acquaintances and be judged like this?

Matthew 7:1-5: "Do not judge, or you too will be judged. For in the same way you judge others, you will be judged, and with the measure you use, it will be measured to you."

Chapter 22
Selling Kindness

We may not be able to make others do what we want, but we can sell them the idea of why they should. Selling an idea is no different than selling merchandise. Our patron first needs to see what we are selling. We then need to show them how it works, prove that it does, and convince them the price tag is a bargain.

We all want people to be kind, loving, and respectful to us, but we cannot demand them. Even if we do, others may not necessarily oblige. These things also lose their very essence when given to us because we requested. Can you imagine how it feels when someone is kind to you just because you asked them to be?

Good relationships make one's life meaningful and happy. We are all social beings who want to be accepted and loved. A relationship involves at least two individuals. For it to be good, there must be a fortuitous and reciprocal flow of kindness and goodwill. Although most people gravitate towards those with similar interests, personalities, or mindsets, sustaining the relationship beyond the honeymoon period requires work. This involves being kind and loving to the other person, so much so that reciprocating would be the easy and natural response. We can change how others act when we change our behavior towards them. Kindness begets kindness. Over time, people mirror what we project to them repeatedly and consistently. That is why we become like the person we interact with the most. We need more people to buy into the idea of kindness if we want to experience more of it.

Ironically, we take those closest to us for granted. We sometimes feel closeness gives us permission to do so. We may even believe the degree of looseness and carelessness of our speech and action determine the depth of the relationship. As if having no boundaries is a mark of true friendship. That is why familiarity often breeds contempt. We wait until the relationship sours before reflecting on why it turned out like this. The people closest to us are the ones we count on to stick with us and accept us when no one would. But how can we expect them to keep loving us when we make it difficult because we do not treat them with basic kindness and respect? We would have nothing to withdraw if we did not invest goodwill in others. It is paramount that we treat the people closest to us with utmost care. They should be treated like precious gems because they are. We need to be thoughtful and speak kindly to them. The relationship should be fun, but we should not make fun of each other. We can make fun of a situation, but never the person. There should be no room for a harsh exchange of words. This would be like leaving a Rolex watch in a gym bag that is thrown around and left unattended on the floor; it will get ruined or stolen. Harsh language can damage a relationship even if it seems innocent and funny at the moment. It is like an alkaline burn that penetrates the surface and necrotizes beneath where the eyes can see. We should consciously treat those dearest to us in a way that reflects how we truly feel about them. It should be evident to them they are special to us. If not, we should contemplate how we can improve. One of the twelve universal laws is the *law of cause and effect* which states that our action will lead to a reaction. If we are kind to others, they will respond kindly to us, born out of the good feeling our kindness generated in them. Another universal law is the *law of compensation* which maintains that we get what we give. We feel good when we are kind to others because we feel noble when our actions make others happy. We feel appreciated and useful when we receive a heartfelt "thank you" for helping someone. Being kind to others may require effort, but it becomes second nature if we continue to practice it. The return on investment is high, and we receive compounding benefits. We will learn that it feels good to be good to others, which encourages us to repeat the behavior. The more we give, the better we feel.

We are all unique individuals and need to learn to accept each other. Sometimes though, we wish that people close to us develop certain traits and characteristics to help improve our relationship. None of us are perfect, and there are always things on which we can improve. Telling someone to do what is not in their nature is ineffective and may be potentially damaging. We do not enter a relationship hoping to change someone. Two people come together because they are compatible and see something they like in each other. It is mutually beneficial to help each other grow and become better. If we wish someone to be more thoughtful, loving, considerate, or kind, we need to give them a sample of what it is like. It may be in our nature to be like that, but it is not theirs. We cannot presume that they have it in them to be so. It requires an adequate experience of love to be able to love. Selling the idea of kindness is no different from selling ice cream. The color and texture may look good, but everyone has preferences. Some do not like it too sweet, and some may want it plain. We let people sample what we have to offer and let them experience it for themselves. If they enjoy the experience, they will come back for more. Once they have acquired a taste for it, they may not just buy it for themselves, but may also start sharing it with others. If we want others to act in a certain way, be that way to them first and let their experience convince them that it is good. The effort required to be kind is minimal if it is in your nature. If you honestly believe in the quality and benefits of what you sell, trust that people will buy into it and start being it. That is how we change the world, one person at a time. We change ourselves, and the world will follow.

The best time to sell an umbrella is when it is raining. It is easier to sell the idea of kindness when people are rude and mean to us. It is possible that their behavior is an expression of internal pain and need for love. When people are unkind and we love them anyway, the counter-intuitiveness of it highlights its significance. They may be struggling with insecurities or past hurts. Giving them grace by overlooking their fault helps them experience the profundity of unconditional love. This is the kind of love they need to heal. Once they have experienced this, they are better equipped to give the same to others. The beneficiary of our kindness may also wonder how we can remain kind despite the affront. If asked, we may have a perfect opportunity to share the reason behind our actions, whatever that may be. For sure, it is because of something higher than us. Turning the other cheek may require a lot of mental fortitude, but the rewards are eternal. Some investments we make do not require much effort and risk; the rewards are commensurately modest. Being kind when others are not, especially when they are outright hostile, requires heroic efforts, but the rewards can be immeasurable.

The supply of kindness is somewhat limited, but the demand is great. This drives up the cost of kindness. People sometimes go through extreme measures to find a dose of it. Many people suffer from the lack of it; they live despondent and depressed. Suicide has become a significant problem in modern society because of this. We need to be good salespeople of kindness. We need to hand out "samples" of kindness whenever opportunities present themselves. Let people experience it so they will know the joy it brings to themselves and others. We need to show them how to do it by our example. Hopefully, they will pass it on to the next person they meet. There is a price to pay for anything good in life. Fostering love and kindness in our daily lives requires sacrifice and effort. Others paid the price for us, and we must pay it forward to keep this good thing going. We cannot do all the work ourselves. We need to recruit more people to buy in and help spread the word. By this, we all end up experiencing more kindness when there is an abundance of it overflowing and pervading various sectors of society. Help sell kindness. When people buy one, you take one.

"When people are unkind and we love them anyway, the counter-intuitiveness of it highlights its significance."

PART VIII: SEEKING A FORGIVING HEART

Dear God,

Why is it so hard for me to forgive others

when I need so much of it myself?

Remind me of my iniquities so that I may be humbled.

Give me the kind of heart that finds it easy to forgive.

Chapter 23
The Heart of the Prodigal's Dad

We find meaning and purpose in life when we do something to benefit others, especially if it involves sacrifice and there is nothing for us to gain. When driven by this, we get an extra energy boost to persevere through fatigue, resistance, and disappointments. The opportunity to speak for those who do not have a voice, listen to those who feel unheard, sit beside those who have no one, and give hope to those who have none, motivates me and gives me a reason to take on life full throttle. The adrenaline rush derived from serving others can be addicting though, and sometimes, we unconsciously seek this instead of pursuing the original intention of pleasing God. If we are not careful, this selfless act of serving others can ironically become a selfish indulgence of the ego. This is why we still feel empty and without peace despite living a life of service. "... *if I have faith that can move mountains, but do not have love, I am nothing. If I give all I possess to the poor and give over my body to hardship that I may boast, but do not have love, I gain nothing.*" 1 Corinthians 13: 2-3.

Presuming we serve others out of pure selfless love, the highest form of purposeful living, our lives can still feel incomplete. We may find meaning in our existence, but still struggle to find lasting peace. The kind of love we give when serving others may not be the all-encompassing love that pleases God. In 1 Corinthians 13:4-7, St. Paul said, "*Love is patient, love is kind. It does not envy, it does not boast, it is not proud. It does not dishonor others, it is not self-seeking, it is not easily angered, it keeps no record of wrongs. Love does not delight in evil but rejoices with the truth. It always protects, always trusts, always hopes, always perseveres.*" He laid out for us what love is and what it is not. He described the kind of love that reflects God's true nature. We may be patient and kind to the people we are serving, but boastful, condescending, proud, envious, and easily angered towards the people we serve alongside with. One negates the other, leaving us feeling empty and unfulfilled because partial obedience to God is disobedience just the same. Selective or limited loving is not what God expects from us. As a result, we continue to long for that elusive sense of satisfaction. I once thought that serving God by serving others would put me right with Him and earn me lasting joy. Sometimes, this does not happen. I realized that when I was impatient, unkind, selfish, short-tempered, judgmental, and held grudges when serving, I failed to experience the happiness I expected and felt unfulfilled. It was apparent I did not love enough. Learning to love adequately is a process that requires prayer, time, and practice. Until we achieve it, circumstances and other people's behaviors will control how we feel, act, and behave. Our love will become conditional.

We are always a work in progress. Our lifelong goal is to learn how to love genuinely. We need to experience love, to know how to love. Fortunately, God loved us first and showed us how. Seeking to love perfectly is not the goal; it is impossible and unnecessary. Our goal should be to have a heart that strives to love better daily. We should be unrelenting in pursuing this and constantly challenge ourselves to do what we must, even if it is uncomfortable and difficult.

In Luke 15:11-32, Jesus told the parable of the prodigal son. There was a man who had two sons, and the younger one left his father's household and misused his inheritance in reckless living. He lost everything he had and became desperate. He returned to his father seeking forgiveness and an opportunity to work even as a hired servant. His father not only welcomed him back with open arms, but also celebrated his return. The older son was upset about his father's underappreciation of his model behavior. Furthermore, he perceived his father's generosity towards his brother, whom he rewarded despite his recklessness, as favoritism. But the prodigal son's father remained unfazed and did not mind his older son's disapproval. He was simply happy and thankful his wayward son had returned home.

In this parable, Jesus illustrated for us the kind of heart that pleases God through the prodigal son's father. His response to both of his sons demonstrated pure and unconditional love. It is a heart that gives and forgives and is willing to give up being right in exchange for the opportunity to love and make peace. This encapsulates all the characteristics and facets of love we should strive to learn to give. Whenever we have an opportunity or have it within our power to give, we must give. Whenever we need to forgive, even when the offending party does not ask for it, we must forgive. When someone asks for it, we must forgive even if we are upset and do not feel the other person deserves it. This mindset and attitude of reflexive giving and forgiving take practice to be better at doing. We can learn to do anything if we spend time and try; it does not matter how long it takes to get there. We should welcome every opportunity and challenge to give and forgive. Soon, our ability to muster the strength to do it becomes second nature. We should not live in fear of failing to live up to our intentions; perfection is not the goal. Making mistakes or falling into sin is unavoidable despite our best efforts. We should commit to always do our best and persevere in making incremental progress towards transforming ourselves into someone who can give and forgive at will.

God commissioned us to love, not to be right. It does not please Him if we are right but fail to love. It is not worth it to demand what we deserve or what is due us if the tradeoff is losing our peace or giving up an opportunity to be kind. In the Sermon on the Mount (Matthew 5: 9), Jesus said, *"Blessed are the peacemakers, for they will be called children of God."* When people formulate an incorrect opinion or judge us unfairly, giving up our right to defend ourselves yields unfathomable satisfaction. When we say, *"I'm sorry,"* even if it is not necessary, but we say it anyway for the sake of peace, we will gain more gratification than the pride we stand to lose. When others want to take what is rightfully ours, consider just letting them have it if we have allowances; God gave us extra provisions for contingencies like this. When people mistreat us despite our good intentions, give them time to realize their mistake and do not be too quick to write them off as they deserve. We should not wager our peace on seeking what is right in man's eyes. Instead, we should be proud we had the strength to deny ourselves and dared to love others radically even at a cost.

The issue of loving others is less formidable towards the disadvantaged or those in dire need. We serve them enthusiastically and are usually patient and kind without exerting extra effort. Often, we also do not expect anything in return. It makes us feel good and proud to help those in need. This is possible because we somehow feel more blessed and superior. The challenge is loving the people close to us who do not feel the need to put their best behavior on display, and those we casually encounter in our everyday lives whom we do not know well enough to feel obligated to love beyond the bare minimum of human decency. The people we work with, acquaintances, and ordinary unnamed people we interact with superficially in our mundane existence are the ones that will truly test our ability to love unconditionally. Succeeding in giving and forgiving in these circumstances will satisfy the most. These are the moments when we answer the call of God to love genuinely, when no one is watching and there is no recognition or reward to gain.

In all matters, whether big or small, complex, or ordinary, the example of the prodigal son's father will teach us how to love unconditionally. He is imperfect like us, but he is always willing to give and forgive. He seeks the things that have eternal value and chooses to love while giving up the need to be right. This is what pleases God. Consequently, this leads to true and lasting happiness, contentment, and inner peace.

"God commissioned us to love, not to be right. It does not please Him if we are right but fail to love."

Chapter 24
I Forgive You Because I Need Forgiveness Too

We do not have much power or control over anything in this world. We are not guaranteed good health just because we eat well, take vitamins, and stay away from sick people. We cannot "make" children just because we are ready to have them. Doctors cannot truly heal a patient; they can prescribe antibiotics but that does not always eradicate the infection. We can be determined, diligent, and passionate, but success does not always follow. Our only absolute power in this life is the ability to forgive. We alone hold the power to determine if we would forgive someone and when. We can make this decision independent of whether the other person deserves or asks for it. No one can force us to forgive, and no one can stop us from forgiving. Even the most powerful ruler in this world cannot outmatch this power that we alone hold. Every single day, we have hundreds of interactions with various people. It is not difficult to encounter someone who would offend, betray, or neglect us. Hence, there are many daily opportunities to exercise our one true power.

There are a lot of things I want to change about myself. Try as I may, I still fail more often than I succeed. In his letter to the Romans, St. Paul echoed precisely how I feel. He said, "*I want to do what is right, but I can't. I want to do what is good, but I don't. I don't want to do what is wrong, but I do it anyway* (Romans 7:18-19)." The recurring reminders of my human frailty keep me humble. They taught me not to put unreasonable expectations on others. I have often been shown grace when I was less than lovable. Who am I then to lord it over others when their human nature got the better of them? Thank God, over the years, I have become more forgiving and happier as a result. I find it more satisfying to forgive than bear the burden of a grudge. We all make mistakes despite our best efforts. We want to say the right things, but sometimes, we still say something unwise and offensive. We want to be thoughtful, but sometimes, we get busy and forget the people who really matter to us. Let us just live and let live. Let us be quick to forgive just as we have been forgiven. In Matthew 7:3, Jesus said, *"Why worry about a speck in your friend's eye when you have a log in your own?"* When we cannot even make ourselves do the right thing with full control of our own actions, how can we expect to exert force over the thoughts and actions of others, with their own autonomy? When confronted with situations where change is needed, it is better to just focus on what we can and should do. We should avoid the hamster wheel trap where we dwell on what others are doing wrong or not doing and try to change them to no avail.

When others are being judgmental and unfair, we should focus solely on ensuring that we do not behave the same way towards them. Hopefully, our unconventional response to their mistreatment will inspire them to change. When someone we have loved deeply loves us only superficially, we should not withhold love when it is required. We can only control what we give and should let God determine what we receive. When someone does not invest the same effort in a relationship, we should continue to add value to it and hope our solo effort is enough to sustain it. If this were not enough, the relationship would eventually wither and die, and the problem would take care of itself. When we wonder why some people choose to live in the dark, remember that we were once there. During those times, others were patient and loving toward us, and gave us time to find the light on our own. Consider the possibility that loving unconditionally may be the better approach. When we are overwhelmed with the injustices, poverty, and sufferings surrounding us and wonder where God is and what everyone is doing about them, we should ask ourselves, *"Is this not why God gave me life and put me here on earth?"*

Even if I know I am entitled to something, I do not necessarily need to lay claim to it; I can choose to be generous and relinquish what is mine. Even if I know I am right, I do not necessarily need to make the people around me feel they are wrong; not everything wrong is consequential. Even if I have the strength and the skills to crush those who seek to destroy me, I can decide to walk away and not say a word; sometimes no response is the best defense. Sometimes, giving up something is the more effective way to gain peace and genuine happiness in return. In your lifetime, you must have tried the "an eye for an eye, and a tooth for a tooth," "what is mine is mine," and "what is right is right" approaches. Where did that get you? If the status quo failed you before, why not try a different approach? It is said in Romans 12:17-18, 20-21, "*Never pay back evil with more evil. Do things in such a way that everyone can see you are honorable. Do all that you can to live in peace with everyone. If your enemies are hungry, feed them. If they are thirsty, give them something to drink. In doing this, you will heap burning coals of shame on their heads. Don't let evil conquer you but conquer evil by doing good.*"

PART IX: SEEKING OUR TRUE IDENTITY

Dear God,

Sometimes, I rely on others to tell me who I am,

or let my successes, failures, and mistakes define me.

I feel confused and insecure.

Tell me who You say I am and why you put me here.

Give me faith to obey and courage to carry out Your will.

CHAPTER 25
FINDING WHO WE REALLY ARE

I f we know who we really are and our purpose in life, we will feel more secure, and our lives will be more meaningful. Our happiness would not depend on others or circumstances, and our actions would be focused and resolute. It is analogous to a company needing to know what its mission is. Its leaders need to remember why it was created in the first place. The type of business may be obvious, but its vision needs to be stated. I helped start our medical practice. What we do is obvious, but why we do what we do and how we plan to do things need to be clearly expressed. This led me to come up with our slogan: *"Get the treatment you need, and the service you deserve."* We want to provide our patients with the best doctors to help them with their ailments, but we value the importance of customer service in the healing process. In our mission statement, we also affirmed our intention of treating our employees like family, and hopefully, they will treat our patients the same way.

When asked to say something about ourselves, we often tell people what we do for a living or recite our awards and achievements. It is as if our identity is based on them. We say, *"I am a doctor"* or *"I am a national champion."* This is acceptable and is the norm in the practical aspect of life. However, for us to find true happiness, purpose, and peace in life, we need to seek our real identity and remind ourselves of it. If my identity is based on being a doctor, what happens after I retire? If my identity is based on being a national champion, what happens when people forget what I have accomplished? Some people base their identity on their physical beauty. What happens when they age, and no cosmetic interventions could reverse it? Basing our identity on superficial, fleeting, and worldly things would undoubtedly end in disappointment. They do not last, and we will be left feeling worthless.

I once looked in the mirror and asked myself who I really was. I am aware that my person consists of a body and soul. My soul is who I truly am. It consists of my personality and that part of me that feels, thinks, and loves. It is that part of me that communicates with God when I pray. It is that part of me that connects with other people without the help of words. It is that part of me that is moved by the beauty of art, music, and literature. So, I stared at the image in the mirror and looked straight into my eyes. The flesh of my body and the adornments attached to it faded from my consciousness. Then all I was aware of was me. I was in touch with my soul, the part of me I cannot touch or see and can only know and understand. Through my eyes, I saw the very essence of the person I know is me. If you were to ask me to state who I believe I truly am, I would say, *"I am God's child," "I am God's creation,"* and *"I am God's servant."* That is who I truly am, my true and lasting identity.

I am God's child because Jesus said in Matthew 6:9, *"This, then, is how you should pray: 'Our Father in heaven: May your holy name be honored."* I am calling God my father because I am His child. Knowing that I am God's child gives me comfort and security. I know I am loved, and there is someone who will always provide for my needs and safeguard me from all harm. Because I am a child, it would be fitting for me to be obedient and follow my father's will. Like an uninitiated child, I may try to exercise my independence and do things my way or on my own and end up in trouble, but that is how I learn. I am a father to my children, and I know a father will always give and forgive. Because I am only a child, I am dependent on my father. That is what my father wants. Jesus said in John 15:4-5, *"Remain in me, as I also remain in you. No branch can bear fruit by itself; it must remain in the vine. Neither can you bear fruit unless you remain in me. I am the vine; you are the branches. If you remain in me and I in you, you will bear much fruit; apart from me you can do nothing."* And that, I will try to do.

I am God's creation. Psalm 139:13 says, *"For you created my inmost being; you knit me together in my mother's womb."* I was designed by God the way He wanted me to be. I have imperfections by human standards, but God must have thought He did a perfect job when He made me; that is all that matters. Jesus said in John 15:16, *"You did not choose me, but I chose you and appointed you so that you might go and bear fruit."* God knew what He wanted when He created me. My personality traits and human tendencies may lead me to make inevitable mistakes, but I know this would not surprise God. Because of this, I will enjoy who I am; nothing about me is a mistake. I will apologize for my mistakes but will not express regret for being imperfect. There are things about me that need to be improved, but even that is part of God's grand plan. If all God created were perfect individuals, what would life here on earth be for? I am always a work in progress, a life under construction. I will maximize my potential without feeling disappointed about things I cannot do. I was not born with the knowledge and talent to do everything and will not insist otherwise. God only expects me to work hard, persevere, and do my best in every endeavor.

I am God's servant. God has been very kind and generous to me. He has given me more than I deserve. He loves me despite my shortcomings. He always forgives me even if I say, *"I'm sorry,"* and do the very same thing the next day. He always welcomes me even after I walked away and pretended that I did not know Him, only to return when I needed something. He always helps and comforts me even when I cannot find the words, do not have the strength, or am too proud or ashamed to ask Him. How can I not dedicate my life to serving Him after all He has done for me? In 1 John 4:19, it is said that *"We love because He first loved us."* What can I offer God to show my gratitude? Only my love and obedience would mean anything to Him. The German philosopher Friedrich Nietzsche once said, *"He who has a Why to live for can bear almost any How."* Serving God by serving others is the highest purpose one can have in life. This lends meaning to life and helps us bear the difficulties we face. Ultimately, this will help us find contentment, peace, and true happiness in life. As Viktor Frankl, an Austrian psychiatrist who wrote the famous book *Man's Search for Meaning*, said *"Happiness cannot be pursued; it must ensue, and it only does so as the unintended side-effect of one's dedication to a cause greater than oneself or as the by-product of one's surrender to a person other than oneself."*

After all these years, I finally found who I truly am. I am God's child. I am God's creation. I am God's servant. Because of this, I found security and peace, and learned to love myself and others more.

Chapter 26
What is Your Life Anchored To?

I am alone in the middle of the ocean. The wind is blowing, and the waves are crashing on me. For a moment, I am underwater and thank God I can rise again to catch my breath. I desperately hold on to a piece of the broken boat; there is nothing else on which to hold. This battle with wind and water is wearing me down. These forces of nature carried me away farther into the darkness. Holding on to the remnant of the boat keeps me afloat, but I cannot keep myself from drifting off further into nothingness.

Have you ever been in a situation where you hold on to something to keep you from falling, but you fall anyway because you grabbed onto something not firmly planted? This is what happens when we anchor ourselves to something or someone other than God. God is the only one constantly faithful to us and unchanging. He is who He says He is and does not change with our changing attitude towards Him or the progression of time. In Psalms 91:1-2, 4, it says: *"Whoever dwells in the shelter of the Most High will rest in the shadow of the Almighty. I will say of the Lord, 'He is my refuge and my fortress, my God, in whom I trust.' He will cover you with his feathers, and under his wings you will find refuge; his faithfulness will be your shield and rampart."*

We believe in things that we can see, hear, and touch. The concept of God is abstract, and some find it hard to hold on to something they consider a figment of their imagination. Sometimes, our conversations with God are attributed by some as made-up thoughts derived from wishful thinking. The problem with things we can see, hear, and touch is that they do not last. Relying on them for security is like holding on to a broken piece of a boat in the middle of the ocean to guide us back to shore. We need to anchor ourselves and our lives to something permanent and unchanging. Hopefully, through the eyes of faith, we find this in God.

What do we anchor our lives to? It is important to figure this out and adjust our thoughts and priorities as needed. What, where, and who do we run to when in dire straits? What or who motivates us to do what we do? What or who gives us a sense of purpose and meaning in life? The answer to these questions will reveal what our lives are anchored to.

Wealth and success, friendships and relationships, good health and fitness, and worldly pleasures have one thing in common: they are all transient and fleeting. They can be here today and gone before tomorrow comes. They are unreliable and ever-changing, and we cannot control them. It is not wise to invest all our energy in them and hope to feel secure. We have all been there and done that, and if we are honest with ourselves, we will admit that they did not live up to the hype. It is a sobering truth. In Matthew 6:19-21, Jesus said, *"Do not store up for yourselves treasures on earth, where moths and vermin destroy, and where thieves break in and steal. But store up for yourselves treasures in heaven, where moths and vermin do not destroy, and where thieves do not break in and steal. For where your treasure is, there your heart will be also."*

It is not wrong to make good use of our time and talent and be the best that we can be. In fact, that is the will of God. We may find wealth and success in the process, but we should acknowledge God as the source of all these. We are to use God's gifts to serve those He placed in our lives. God gave us friends and relationships to keep us company, make us happy, encourage, and enlighten us. He also gave us good health and the ability to experience worldly pleasures because He loves us and wants us to enjoy the life He gave us. It is not wrong to cherish all these gifts from God. In fact, I am sure that is what God wants. Would anyone give a gift and wish the recipient not to delight in it? However, we should not become intoxicated by these and make them our pseudo-Gods. They should be mere reminders of God's goodness, generosity, and love for us. We should be grateful for the gifts and honor the giver. Sometimes, God has no choice but take them away to remind us of this and keep us from destroying ourselves with what He meant for our good.

So, what or who should we anchor our lives to? We need to anchor our lives to something that lasts and is worthy of our devotion and energies. We need to anchor our lives to someone whose love and loyalty do not change depending on his circumstances or our attitude. We need to anchor our lives to someone whose character is beyond reproach and does not change. In Colossians 3:2, St. Paul said, *"Set your minds on things above, not on earthly things."* We must anchor our lives to God and devote our days pleasing Him and doing His will. Only then will we find peace, security, and lasting happiness.

CHAPTER 27
THE BATTLE WITHIN

We are all created in the image of God. Therefore, there is both a God nature and human nature within us. Because we are human, it takes less effort to obey the latter. When someone insults us, it is more natural to retort with sarcasm. It often feels good to do so, at least at that moment. We do or consume many things because they provide temporary pleasure, even if we know what unpleasant consequences await us on the other side. There is always a battle within us between our God nature and human nature. Our lives would be happier and trouble-free if we let our God nature dominate. What springs out of our God nature is what the Bible refers to as the "fruits of the Spirit" in Galatians 5:22; these are love, joy, peace, patience, kindness, goodness, self-control, gentleness, and faithfulness. St. Augustine said, *"Conquer yourself and the world lies at your feet."* Once we conquer our human nature, the world indeed lies at our feet. We can do what we know leads to true and lasting happiness and contentment. The only way to win this battle is to feed our minds with thoughts that nurture our God nature. In Philippians 4:8, the Bible instructs us to think of these things -- *"whatever is true, whatever is noble, whatever is right, whatever is pure, whatever is lovely, whatever is admirable, and anything that is excellent or praiseworthy."* Our heart's desires are born out of the thoughts that fill our minds. The mouth then speaks what the heart is full of. We eventually believe and find true the things about which we most often speak. Our beliefs then form our habits and behaviors. I make time to pray regularly. I pray often NOT because I am holy but because I MUST win this battle between my God nature and human nature.

Part X: Seeking More Faith

Dear God,

The storms of life overwhelm me.

The harder I try, the more frustrated I become.

I take one step forward and slide back two or more.

Help me have more faith; show me how.

CHAPTER 28
FAITH JOURNEY

Living a life of faith in the public eye is difficult. We all go through tough times in life that we refer to as trials. Looking at it through the lens of faith, many believe God uses them to teach us, strengthen us, and grow our faith. These life events are challenging, and we must suffer, succumb, and try to recover as the world watches us in our most vulnerable moments. We want to keep our composure, but if God were to achieve His objectives, He must push us to the breaking point to mold us. In other words, we will surely fall, and this will happen for the world to see. The redemptive part of this is what we do when we fall; that is also for the world to see. That is the part where we can either draw people to God or turn people away from Him. Falling is not the problem; not getting up is. Having this insight will help us not to fear failure. What we need to fear is the fear of facing difficult situations because we are afraid to fail. Our growth happens when we struggle to bounce back from our failures.

It is hard enough to go through trials in life, but uncertainty exacerbates their effects. It is like being lost in the middle of the ocean without a frame of reference for the shore. We might give up any hope of surviving, only to discover we are a few miles away from land. I have gone through many trials in my life. God never promised a life without suffering. But He did promise that He would help us through them. Over the years, I have noticed a pattern I go through as I faced the many trials God allowed. Knowing what to expect helped comfort me and gave me the stamina to hang in there until God's plan fully unfolded.

Here are the ten stages of a faith journey we may experience as we go through some of life's most difficult challenges:

1. Realizing we are in a storm.
Life is calm and good, and we are enjoying the status quo. Suddenly, some life event hits us out of nowhere, often unexpected. It catches us off guard and unprepared. Life seems out of control as we struggle to comprehend what is happening.

2. Experiencing the storm.
We are pummeled from all sides. Before we can recover from the first, another blow comes. There seems to be no end in sight. We are down on our knees, and then motionless on our back. We looked around and saw no one. It is wet, cold, and dark.

3. Praying for help and asking others to intercede.
We know we have a strong faith in God; at least, we thought we did based on our past experiences and how we lived our life. We call on God who is ever faithful to us. We are surrounded by friends who are similarly devoted to God. Together, we ask God to stop the storm, or at least give us peace and courage as we face it. We all pray fervently.

4. Asking God, "Why?"
It has been a while now. God seems silent. We know He has a purpose for allowing this storm in our lives, but we cannot figure out what. We know He is with us, but we cannot feel His presence. We keep praying but we cannot hear His voice. We are getting weak and exhausted, and all we can utter to God is, *"Why?"*

5. Asking God, "When?"; "When will you help us?" and "When will this end?"
We are trying desperately to hold on to our faith and not waver. The spirit is willing, but our flesh is failing. We are not sure we can hold on any longer. We know God would not give us more than we can handle. We know God will provide us with a way out at the opportune time. We know He is aware of what we are enduring and has a plan. But we wonder, how much longer will this continue? When will God show up and save us, especially when we do His will and serve Him? Why do people who do the right thing have to suffer so much? We know that God is just, but when will He intervene? We believe

that surely, He will not allow this to destroy us. We recall His promise in the scriptures that *"no weapon formed against you shall prosper* (Isaiah 54:17)."

6. Trusting God.

We are tired of wrestling God and decided to be still and let God be God. We know we can trust Him; besides, we do not have a choice at this time. We cannot control others, and we cannot control our circumstances. We are not smart enough to know what else to do and not strong enough to keep fighting. We are glad we know God and have nurtured a relationship with Him. It is like we have deposited money in the bank and now have something from which to draw. We surrender everything to Him and submit to His will. A sudden calm envelops us, and we can rest. Suddenly, we feel His presence, and hear His voice.

7. Marveling at God's interventions.

The storm begins to wane; the waves cease as if commanded. Things miraculously start to change. We are beginning to see a sliver of light on the horizon. A new day is about to begin. God rewarded us double for our struggles and we received more than what we lost. We are in awe. We never thought this day would come.

8. Feeling embarrassed that we doubted.

We thought we had a strong faith; this trial exposed our lack of it. We are embarrassed. We feel unworthy for doubting the goodness of God. We beat up ourselves over this but eventually decided to learn from it instead. We realize that questioning is part of the faith journey.

9. Enlightenment; realizing the wisdom, strength, and faith gained.

After all the beating, we are wounded. But the wounds begin to heal, and the pain is gone. We formed scars; they are tougher than normal skin. We gained wisdom. Our faith is stronger, but surely, there is still more room to grow. We know there will be another trial coming to help take us to the next level. We know God will not let us settle into complacency. The only way for us to continue growing is for Him to keep stirring us up.

10. Telling others about it.

We are in awe of what we experienced. God is truly amazing and praiseworthy. We experienced God's love, power, and faithfulness because we suffered. The joy we felt was overwhelming; it was too much to contain. We could not help but share our story with the next person we encounter. We became the messenger God sent to that person who happened to be going through his own storm.

This is the faith lifecycle; we suffer, we pray, we grow, and repeat. This cycle will continue until we become who God wants us to be. There is redemptive value in suffering. It leads us to seek God and, in the process, transforms us. It helps peel off layers that separate us from God, like good health, success, and a happy family life. All these blessings can make us feel self-sufficient. They can mislead us to believe we can live a life independent from God. Suffering is a very effective tool God can use to mold us and prepare us for the work He needs us to do.

"There is redemptive value in suffering. It leads us to seek God and, in the process, transforms us."

CHAPTER 29
GOOD SAMARITANS

C oming home from an extended trip, we found our car at the airport parking garage with a flat tire and dead battery. After being in an airplane for over twenty-one hours and our body's internal clock was out of sync with the new time zone, my family and I were tired and ready to go home. This was indeed a bummer. Somehow, I remained calm and reminded myself that everything happens for a reason, and believed God allowed this to happen to protect or teach us something. I made a few phone calls to see who might be able to help, but unfortunately, no one was available at the time. There must be someone at the airport who could help, I reckon. This was a small airport, and I knew the man who owned the airport transportation service company. He had given my family rides to and from the airport many times before. When I asked him for help, he said he could not but knew someone at the airport who could. This very kind gentleman left his work area and walked around the airport with me, looking for the airport shuttle driver he knew who had the equipment. Luckily, we found her, and she was very nice and more than happy to assist. I explained to her our car was parked on the third floor of the parking garage, and she told me she would meet me there with the necessary equipment. She had to drop off the shuttle bus she was driving at the time and pick up a different vehicle to drive to us. In the meantime, I returned to our car and waited patiently. In less than ten minutes, a white van passed, driven by a lady who resembled the one I spoke with previously. I thought, with all she told me she had to do before meeting us, I was surprised at how fast she arrived. I waved at the van driver, and she abruptly stopped. I then realized she was not who I was expecting. Nonetheless, this lady was as nice and asked me if I needed anything. I explained my situation and she was able to help jumpstart our car battery, but unable to inflate the tire. Eventually, the first lady arrived and inflated my tire, and we were good to go. I told her she was God-sent, and we all thanked her profusely.

When we finally arrived home, we discovered our air conditioning system, Wi-Fi, garage door, sprinkler system, and refrigerator were not working. They were likely damaged by a local storm two days prior. The house was very warm, and I had to get emergency help. I called several heating and air companies in town, but none could assist that night. One of them put us on the waiting list for emergency technician support but told us it would likely be two days before someone would be available. We were tired from our trip but could not rest in this heat. The following day, I got a call from someone at the heating and air company who said that one of their clients canceled their appointment and that a technician could come to our house immediately if we were available. Someone came and restored the air conditioning in some areas of the house but needed to order parts to fix the others. The technician was extremely kind, thorough, and helpful. He was genuine in his desire to assist us and keen to diagnose the problem. A little later, my good friend's uncle offered to send his computer technician to help inspect and fix our Wi-Fi. In this modern-time, Wi-Fi is necessary for basic living, and I needed it badly to catch up with work. This technician gave up his family time on a Friday night to come help us. He had promised his son they would paint his room that night, but instead, spent four hours serving our needs. A colleague of mine also later heard we needed help, so he came by to inspect our sprinkler system, garage door, and refrigerator and helped get the process started in getting them fixed. During all this, my wife did not feel well, and we were very thankful my doctor friend took my call early the next morning and prescribed the appropriate medicine.

As I went through these consecutive, unexpected nightmares, there seemed to be no end in sight. It felt like everything was conspiring to take me down. Even though the emergencies were addressed, we still had a long way to go in achieving normalcy. I am thankful I kept my faith believing that God intended all these for our good, and He had plans greater than what I could see at the time. But until a friend texted to encourage me, I was focused on the idea that God allowed all the unpleasant things to happen. As if God was saying, "I love you, son; you need to be tortured for your own good, so here it is." My friend reminded me it was the devil who inflicted our pain and misery; the same devil who destroys things and relationships and tries to draw us away from God by leaving us despondent. Although God may have allowed our suffering to transform, sanctify, and teach us, He was not the one who caused the chaos and destruction. I should have turned my attention instead to the fact it was God who sent the Good Samaritans we met along the way and helped us overcome the challenges we encountered. He provided us with a way out of our dire circumstances and protected us against the evil forces that sought to discourage us. Through all this, God was present at every turn as we navigated through our crisis. He was constantly with us; he kept us calm and secure. It was God who provided all our needs at the time: my encounter with the owner of the airport transportation service company, the airport shuttle driver, the unknown female driver who happened to pass by, the heating and air technician, the computer engineer who fixed our Wi-Fi, my colleague who came by our house to help, my doctor friend who helped take care of my wife, and my friend who texted to encourage and remind me of all this. Not only did these people help us, but they were also extremely nice and caring and made sacrifices for us; we felt the presence of God through them. What happened to our family was inconvenient, but certainly not life-threatening and nothing compared to what many of you are going through. Nevertheless, it was overwhelming because they were consolidated in timeframe and could have easily caused us to question our faith and doubt God. This skepticism may seem harmless, but if allowed to linger, it can lead to a gradual spiritual decline. They are like leaks in the house that cannot be ignored because they will result in costly damage in due time. We need to be always prepared by praying and studying God's word to enable us to put-up appropriate defenses to guard against despair promptly. Through all this, I found peace as I thanked God for the Good Samaritans He provided amid our crises. I was also able to rest assured in knowing that although God allowed them in my life for His higher purpose, He did not inflict them on me or cause them to happen.

Chapter 30
You Never Know

Are you waiting to hear from God about a prayer? Are you hurting and wondering if the pain will ever go away? Have you been wanting to make a change but getting tired of trying? Are you waiting for someone who walked away to return? Have you been praying for someone to change their ways or have a change of heart because that is all you can do? Do you wish that one day you could forgive someone or be forgiven? Are you lonely and praying that God will direct someone your way? Have you been sick and waiting on God for healing? Are you waiting for God to restore a broken relationship? Are you still hoping to be redeemed and vindicated? Are you waiting for that day when you wake up and suddenly realize that what used to haunt you no longer controls you?

Waiting on God can be hard, but not having a God to wait on is tragic. Suffering, hurt, disappointment, loss, and frustrations are part of our human existence together with their counterparts. They are as normal as taking a breath in and out. To truly live our lives to the fullest, we need to accept and engage suffering as much as we enjoy and cherish the joys of life. You cannot have one and not the other. In the same way we understand light because of darkness, see black because of white, and know what heat feels like because of cold, suffering enhances our experience of the good times.

Negative emotions can be just another experience like the positive ones if we accept and interact with them as if they are meant to co-exist. We suffer when we think we should not experience negative emotions. They do not need to be a destructive element of life. In fact, they can be constructive and redemptive if we view them through a lens of faith and discern their purpose and meaning. It becomes a blessing rather than a punishment. We feel the love of God rather than abandonment and neglect. As was said in Romans 8:28, *"And we know that God causes all things to work together for good to those who love God, to those who are called according to His purpose."* Like many of us may have experienced, there are little splinters in life that cause us a lot of pain even though they are seemingly minor. In 2 Corinthians 12:7-9, St. Paul referred to a nagging nuisance God gave him to keep him humble. *"Therefore, in order to keep me from becoming conceited, I was given a thorn in my flesh, a messenger of Satan, to torment me. Three times I pleaded with the Lord to take it away from me. But he said to me, 'My grace is sufficient for you, for my power is made perfect in weakness.' Therefore, I will boast all the more gladly about my weaknesses, so that Christ's power may rest on me."* Faith leads us to trust that God loves us; His desire is our happiness. He promised to meet all our needs and will never abandon us. Until He achieves His purpose for our lives, He will not relent. In Isaiah 55:10-11, God said, *"As the rain and the snow come down from heaven, and do not return to it without watering the earth and making it bud and flourish, so that it yields seed for the sower and bread for the eater, so is my word that goes out from my mouth: It will not return to me empty, but will accomplish what I desire and achieve the purpose for which I sent it."* God's objective is our sanctification and transformation into the person He wants us to be. Whatever He allows in our lives, He intends to use them to achieve His will.

Because we see purpose in our trials, we find meaning in it. This encourages us to remain patient and gives us strength and courage to persevere. Because we know that allowing suffering is a manifestation of God's love for us, we have hope that in due time, when it has served its purpose, God will promptly pull the thorn from our side. And while we are still in the middle of the restorative and redemptive process of suffering, we know He will be there to comfort us. In Psalm 23:4, David prayed, *"Even though I walk through the darkest valley, I will fear no evil, for you are with me; your rod and your staff, they comfort me."* God said in Isaiah 41:10, *"So do not fear, for I am with you; do not be dismayed, for I am your God. I will strengthen you and help you; I will uphold you with my righteous right hand."*

Faith in God gives us hope. It assures us that we can trust Him completely and surrender all our hurt to Him. As a result, we find rest and peace. Having faith convinces us that letting God direct our steps would be wiser than following our own plans. It gives us confidence that no matter what we face, all will be well in due time. Jesus said in Matthew 5:3, *"Blessed are the poor in spirit, for theirs is the kingdom of heaven."* We experience peace and hope when we stop depending on our own wisdom and strength to find them. They are bestowed on us when we acknowledge that we can do nothing without God and completely depend on Him.

"With the Lord a day is like a thousand years, and a thousand years are like a day (2 Peter 3:8)." God's timing is always perfect. There may be no end in sight as we wait for relief from our suffering. But to God, this is just a fraction of eternity, and His only concern is our growth and molding us into the person He wants us to be. In Isaiah 55:8-9, God said, *"For my thoughts are not your thoughts, neither are your ways my ways. As the heavens are higher than the earth, so are my ways higher than your ways and my thoughts than your thoughts."* Because His ways are not ours, we are sometimes left in awe at what God decides to do or the timing of His actions. We should always trust God's intentions and wait patiently for His will to manifest. In the meantime, we must continue to do our best in whatever we are called to do given the circumstances we face. We must constantly pray for courage, strength, and a grateful heart as we learn from our trials and mature in our faith.

You never know, one day, the pain that paralyzed you may no longer hurt even if you remember the cause. You never know, all the effort and dedication you put into correcting a shortcoming or getting rid of a bad habit may suddenly yield results. You never know, the person who unexpectedly walked away may suddenly show up and return home. You never know, the person you gave up on may amaze you with how he turns his life around. You never know, you may finally be able to forgive the person you never thought you could ever forgive, or you may receive forgiveness from the person who refused to forgive you despite your repeated apologies. You never know, you might find someone who truly values you for a change. You never know, God might heal you even when science gave you no chance to be cured. You never know, God might restore a relationship that ended, or replace it with someone better. You never know, God might redeem or vindicate you in full view of your accusers and defamers and restore your dignity. You never know, you might wake up one day and realize that the memories that haunted you, addictions that enslaved you, hurts that chained you, and realities that entrapped you, no longer have power over you. You never know, today may be the day God decides to relieve you of suffering and restore what you lost. This is not wishful thinking. Every day could be the day. Rome was not built in one day, but God can restore you any day. You just never know.

ALSO BY *TERENCE ANGTUACO, M.D.*

DIVINE INTERVENTION: A STORY OF HEALING, LOVE, AND HOPE

SUMMARY

For thirty consecutive weeks, I journaled some of the yearnings of my soul -- the part of me I cannot touch or see and can only know and understand. I wrote about topics which include the pursuit of inner peace, contentment, and consolation, and touched on the issues of faith, love, forgiveness, self-improvement, and building a better world for us to live in. These were inspired by my personal struggles and stories of people who reached out to me for guidance. My deep desire to serve the Lord by inspiring and encouraging others led to the creation of Luceat Lux Ministries. Writing this is part of my journey in this new vocation. I would like to share with you precious lessons I learned from facing challenges in my everyday life. It is my hope that by reading this you will find the easier path to the light. This book is a gift from my soul to yours.

About the Author

Terence Angtuaco, a Doctor of Medicine specializing in Gastroenterology and Hepatology, practices at Premier Gastroenterology Associates in Little Rock, Arkansas. He recently published his first book, *"Divine Intervention: A Story of Healing, Love, and Hope."* Dr. Angtuaco has also written and published scholarly articles in his medical specialty. He founded Luceat Lux Ministries to inspire, encourage, and serve those in need. The author is married, has three children, and is an avid martial artist and tennis player. You can find more information about Dr. Angtuaco on his website at www. TerenceAngtuacoMD.com.

www.TerenceAngtuacoMD.com

🅕 Terence Angtuaco Writes
🅞 terenceangtuacowrites
𝕏 Terence Angtuaco Writes
🅛 Terence Angtuaco

Printed in the United States
by Baker & Taylor Publisher Services